The Dover Patrol

CAPTAIN CARPENTER
FROM A PHOTO TAKEN IMMEDIATELY AFTER HE RECEIVED THE V.C.

The Dover Patrol

The Royal Navy, the English Channel
and the Zeebrugge Raid during the
First World War by an eyewitness

J. J. Bennett

LEONAUR

The Dover Patrol
The Royal Navy, the English Channel
and the Zeebrugge Raid during the
First World War by an eyewitness
by J. J. Bennett

First published under the titles
The Dover Patrol

Leonaur is an imprint
of Oakpast Ltd

ISBN: 978-1-84677-778-3 (hardcover)
ISBN: 978-1-84677-777-6 (softcover)

http://www.leonaur.com

Contents

Introduction

The author of this book writes with personal knowledge and experience of the work done by the Dover Patrol, which he watched at its difficult and dangerous business.

Its functions were of the highest importance. It had in the first place to guard the great route to France, the main artery of our army on the Western Front, from attack both by German surface craft and submarines. It achieved this task with extraordinary success against a most energetic, brave, and enterprising enemy. In no single instance was a British transport with troops on board assailed by this enemy.

So vigilant was the watch of our navy, so admirably were its measures concerted, that a vast traffic was conducted almost without let or hindrance. Day after day leave boats, transports, vessels with material, ammunition, and supplies, moved to and fro under the convoy of our destroyers, submarines, and aircraft, almost as though there had been no war at a distance of sixty miles, or less, from the excellent German bases in Flanders.

Only the destroyers steaming on the beam, ready for action, and (when the weather permitted) the little airships and seaplanes buzzing overhead, told the chance passenger that not many miles away in strongly fortified ports lurked the enemy's craft incessantly watching for an opportunity to strike. The Germans, as is known from the statements of their submarine commanders, hoped at the outset to cut this line of communications. Their failure to do so was one of their greatest disappointments in the war, and must be ascribed solely to the efficiency of the

British Navy.

A second function, connected with the first, was to close the Straits of Dover against enemy submarines and thus prevent them from running down Channel to the waters near its mouth where they could cruise with deadly result. This was achieved in 1918 at the price of many sacrifices, through the heroism of our drifter and trawler crews, who guarded the great barrage closing the Straits. The fishermen engaged in this work were exposed to great danger from attack by surface craft. Their vessels were poorly armed and ill-fitted to meet the powerful German destroyers. They had to be employed because in the overwhelming demands upon our warship resources more formidable vessels could not be provided.

But they did their work. They accomplished their mission. Towards the summer of 1918 the Straits of Dover had become impassable for any but the boldest and most skilful U-boat commanders, and even of them heavy toll was taken. Thus, before Zeebrugge and Ostend passed into the hands of the Allies, they had become useless to the enemy. The Germans had been paralysed by our naval measures.

A third function, which the navy performed under Vice-Admiral Sir Roger Keyes, was that of closing the holes from which the submarines issued. In some of the most critical hours of the war, the raids on Ostend and Zeebrugge lifted the spirit of the nation and showed it what its glorious sea service could do. I am revealing no secrets when I say that but for peremptory orders the author of this book would have been among the eye-witnesses of those raids and would have shared the perils of the combatants.

In the last months of the naval war the Dover Patrol passed from the defensive to a most determined and resolute offensive. Zeebrugge and Ostend were bombed and bombarded with such assiduity at what price Captain Bewsher's *Bombing of Bruges* tells us that the enemy was given no leisure for attack. These operations will always be a model; the history of them is a brilliant page in our records, to be compared with Nelson's offensive against the invasion flotilla at Boulogne in 1801 for energy and aggressiveness, and of them we may say, in Nelson's words, that "more determined, persevering courage" was never witnessed, and "greater zeal and ardent desire to distinguish themselves by an attack on the enemy was never shown than by all the captains, officers, and crews" of the British vessels engaged.

The power of the German defences was great; the heaviest guns were mounted in rich profusion on the Flanders coast; every device of man was employed by the enemy. Because of this, when we bombarded, our bombardments had to be carried out at long range. This was wise tactics as the whole history of naval war is against engaging forts on land at decisive range with ships. Yet the fortifications never stopped our night onslaughts; and it was a fitting close to this war in the Straits that the King of the Belgians paid his first visit to the recaptured ports in a British war vessel.

H. W. Wilson

Author's Preface

To fall foul of any person or anything is no pleasure to a mild-mannered man, but to fall foul of an armistice is incredibly unfortunate. Yet that has, to some extent, been the fate of the present book, and much as I contemn "authors' prefaces "in the majority of books, one is painfully necessary in the present case.

To apologize for a book is to show faint- heartedness as to its execution, but an apology must be made for the conditions in which this volume appears. The work was projected soon after the glittering events of Zeebrugge and Ostend, and was finished before the cessation of hostilities, but delay followed delay until now the war and the stories of the Belgian coast are grouping themselves in the background of history. The reader realizes that in those breathless days before November 11 there existed a censorship which exercised a certain restraint on the publication of naval writings. I do not quarrel with the censorship. Personally, I think these pages, in view of the circumstances of the time, were gently treated. But there were inevitably a number of details which would have completed the book and which are at present lacking.

The book is not incomplete in the sense that there are gaps in its unfolding of the picture of the "Dover Patrol," but I feel that there are many points which would finish off the canvas, and I ask the reader to consider it a book written in war-time and produced in war-time, and judge it accordingly. Many readers, I am sure, will read Chapter 6 and wonder when they are coming to anything that will identify the immortal submarine. I regret to say they will search in vain. But, as a little later, (chapter 9), they will find a reference to submarine "C 3," they may go on their way rejoicing, for they may rest assured that that boat was the one in question. Of course it is a great deal to ask a reader to do, this darting among my pages, but now he knows the explanation I put my faith in him.

There is one more point to which I would refer now I have my reader face to face and can talk plainly to him. A friend with whom I discussed this book has just said to me, with that tone of kindly criticism which friends adopt and which hurts the most, "People do not want war books now." That is a vague statement which is somewhat difficult to understand.

There must be a great reaction against the reading of war books. That is undoubted, but the reaction will be, to my mind, against the ephemeral books on various aspects of land warfare. Even ephemeral books about the navy, like this one, must tell the reader far more than he realized before. The navy's secrets have been well and truly guarded. There have been comparatively few "war books "about the navy, and that is my excuse for writing at all about the *Dover Patrol*. So few people knew anything whatever about it. And if I have been able to introduce the reader in the smallest way into one of the secrets of Britain's sea-power I shall have gained my reward.

History cannot perish although many of its writers do and with some justification. So that if I have been able to cast a little light on the history of the *Dover Patrol* I am well satisfied.

J. J. B.

CHAPTER 1

The Navy's Front-Line Trench

Without some prefatory account of the Dover Patrol and its activities, any narrative dealing with the attacks upon Zeebrugge and Ostend would be like framing an unfinished picture, since these smashing blows at the enemy were dealt as a result of the Dover Patrol being in existence. They were a manifestation on a superlative scale of its fighting spirit, the quality of which the enemy had tasted often before in smaller actions.

There has been a Dover Patrol practically as long as there has been a war. But the name, whilst a convenient enough one for official purposes, conveys to the general public only the shadowiest notion of what this particular unit of our Fleet is held responsible for in the way of war work. Less, indeed, is known of what the Patrol has done, of what it does for the Allies every day, than of what is expected from it. The view prevalently held of the Dover Patrol as consisting of a number of ships which go out for cruises when they feel inclined to do so, and return to port after they get tired of looking for an enemy who bashfully declines to show himself, errs as widely from truth as anything well could do.

As a matter of actual fact this naval force comprises not one patrol alone, but many. So multifarious are its duties, so important an influence has the efficient way in which they are being performed upon the war along the Western Front, as well as upon conditions in the United Kingdom, that the Dover Patrol will be placed by history alongside the Blockade of Brest as an outstanding instance of what sea-power can do for the nation that holds it and knows how to use rightly this all-potent weapon.

The unit of our Fleet which has its administrative centre at Dover (and that, though not so pithy, is a more adequate description than "patrol," a word which conveys to the popular mind an idea of limitations which do not exist in this case) has many functions to discharge. Upon it falls all the convoy work for the short cross-Channel passages. It has to escort to France the vessels carrying troops there. Officers and men returning to "Blighty" must rely on its minesweepers to keep a clear passage for the leave boat, and upon its agile destroyers to see that argosy of happy souls safely from shore to shore.

Our hospital ships are dependent upon it for protection against murder, hiding ghoulishly beneath the waves. And these are but one part of the responsibilities laid upon it. Much of the stores needed by our armies in France have to be carried from port to port under its guardianship. For nearly every ounce of his rations, for nearly all the uncountable millions of cigarettes he smokes, for much of the clothing he wears; for what he eats himself and for what he "feeds" to "Gerry" in different ways, Thomas Atkins is mainly beholden to the Dover Patrol. And as there are many thousands of tons of military stores passed across Channel every day of the year, convoying munition ships is anything but a light task by itself. Geographical circumstance makes the area within which the Dover Patrol plays vigilant watchdog the most vitally important to the Allies of any stretch where land and water meet.

If the Patrol were less unsleeping, so that the enemy—who does not fail through want of trying—once succeeded in cutting our lines of communication where they cross salt water here, and kept them severed for a short while only, the advantage thus gained would be worth more to him than half a dozen "big pushes" on land. One need not enter upon any long disquisition as to just how and why this would be so. A brief study of the map will explain the matter clearly enough to any person of average intelligence.

But the Dover Patrol is charged with other duties, and many of them, as well as that of acting as a permanent "fatigue party" for our army across the Straits, though that job of itself is no sinecure. There are no little things on the fighting side of this war. Being the sea sentinel keeping immediate watch and ward over the Port of London, what happens within the borders of Patrol affects the daily lives of shore folk in our own country much more closely than the majority of them know.

Probably no man or woman in the metropolis looks upon the Patrol or what it does as being an intimate concern of theirs. They regard it as a section of the Fleet stationed a bit nearer to them than some other sections, but beyond that of no greater importance to them than the far-away Grand Fleet divisions half hidden in the northern mists. Get close up to facts, look them squarely in the face, and one sees what an erroneous conception this is. In a very real sense of the comparison, the ships of the Dover Patrol exercise much the same functions for the benefit of the people of London as do the policemen who walk its streets.

The Patrol has two bases—*viz.* Dover and Dunkirk—and its sphere of influence extends for a considerable direction on either hand of these towns. Whether coming up Channel or down the North Sea, all trading vessels bound for London must make the final stages of their voyage along sea roads regularly policed by the fighting ships of the Patrol and cleared of mines by its trawlers, which are the "street cleansing department" in this important stretch of home waters. If the Patrol did not guard them with both sword and shield these trading vessels would have a very perilous time of it getting into port.

On their way there they have actually to pass under the eyes of the enemy—right close under them too. Zeebrugge and Ostend, once of great value to the enemy as gateways from the canals of Flanders into the North Sea, are now useless to him for that purpose. The attacks made on these places by the Dover Patrol, which are described in later chapters, robbed them of all

15

utility to the Hun as points of issue. But the outer harbours of each still provide convenient anchorage for his torpedo vessels and other light craft. By passing them along the shore behind his minefields the enemy has brought down to Zeebrugge particularly a strong flotilla of his finest destroyers. And there they lie impotent. The Dover Patrol keeps such a close watch upon them that they cannot yet get out to sea in the daytime, and so far, at any rate, have been prevented from making any "tip-and-run" dashes by night.

Nothing would suit our seamen better than for the enemy to come out boldly and fight, but he will not. So the position, as it stands, is just this: all London-bound traffic, all merchantmen using the Straits, pass right under the noses of some thirty odd of the enemy's best destroyers, which, though willing enough to wound, are desperately afraid to strike.

The Hun lies in his lair watching our trading ships go by, like a hungry dog crouched in its kennel with eyes fixed greedily upon a tempting bone that it fears to spring out and seize, knowing that immediately it did so somebody waiting nearby with a big stick would promptly hit it on the head. The Dover Patrol holds the big stick, and is always so ready to use it that the Hun dog, personified by this force of destroyers, dare not put a head outside its lurking-place.

What would be the situation if this wholesome fear of the Patrol had not been driven so deeply into the heart of the enemy? From Ostend or Zeebrugge to the Thames Estuary or the Downs is only a very short run indeed for a fast destroyer. Were the enemy able to make any considerable use of his Belgian ports as bases for raiding our shipping from, as happily he is not, the Downs would soon be emptied, and there would be little or no seaborne trade going in or out of London river.

As it is, merchant-men come and go between London and the world at large, enjoying an immunity from enemy attack that speaks highly for the efficiency of the force which secures this for them. It is well that the people who benefit by it should realize what this phase of the Dover Patrol's work means to our land population; how closely it touches their daily lives; how dependent they are upon it for many things not outstandingly apparent, but the value of which would be recognized immediately they were lost.

And this Patrol acts literally as "Keeper of the Gate." It is common knowledge that except for just one gateway through them, the Straits of Dover are impregnably walled across. By day every cable's length of this barrier is closely watched. By night vigilance redoubles. Huge flares burn along the "wall" in beacon fashion, giving no opportunity for "U" boats to creep through it under cover of darkness. The duty of watching this "wall" and guarding the gate falls upon the Patrol.

CHAPTER 2

The Patrol Goes "Over the Top"

What has been said about preventive measures should not lead one to infer incorrectly that naval strategy in the Patrol area concerns itself wholly with the defensive. Operations of this nature are conducted on an extensive scale because they constitute an essential part of naval war. It is just as vital to protect our own shipping as to destroy that of the enemy.

The geographical position of its territory makes the Dover Patrol, as already stated, the front-line trench of the war by sea, and a considerable part of its activities are of a front-line character. Every day the Patrol comes into fighting touch with the Hun somewhere or other. Offensive tactics have for this long time past filled a big place in its scheme of operations. The chance of a real ding-dong sea-fight occurs but seldom, as the enemy does his utmost to avoid such encounters.

The *Broke* and the *Swift* taught him a lesson. Just after midnight on April 20, 1917, these two destroyer leaders whilst patrolling the Channel fell in with a flotilla of German torpedo craft. It was a calm, intensely dark night. When the enemy were first sighted they were about 600 yards distant, trying to rush past unseen. Failing in this, all along their line gongs boomed orders in response to which the Germans immediately opened fire with every available gun. Captain A. M. Peck, of the *Swift*, our leading ship, gladly accepted the challenge.

Unhesitatingly he swung his ship round and endeavoured to ram the foremost German. By a hand's-breadth or so he missed her. Running down a swiftly moving vessel in an inky-black atmosphere with only momentary gun-flashes as a guide is "chancy" work. On went the *Swift*, straight through the foeman's lines. Spinning round she torpedoed one of his craft, then sprang hot-foot at another.

Terror-stricken lest the *Swift's* sharp bows should find him, this German shut down his guns and fled hurriedly into the darkness. After him raced the *Swift*, keen as a hawk after its quarry. For as long as she could do so with any chance of success the *Swift* pursued. Decreasing speed due to the injuries she had received finally obliged her to break off the chase. So she turned back to seek another opponent.

Whilst nosing about with this end in view, the *Swift* saw the loom of a stationary enemy hull in the blackness ahead of her. Creeping warily towards it, with her guns ready for action, the *Swift* came finally upon an extraordinary scene. The German boat was sinking. Her crew had mustered on deck, and were shouting in chorus: "We surrender! We surrender!" Knowing how little the word of a Hun may be relied upon, the *Swift* approached cautiously, in case this "white flag" declaration masked some intended act of treachery.

Whilst the *Swift* was picking her way warily towards them the Germans ceased shouting. Quite suddenly their vessel heeled slowly over—and sank. Certain at last that no trap had been laid for her, the *Swift* switched on her searchlights, lowered her boats and set about the work of picking up the German sailors from the water.

Meanwhile, her consort, the *Broke*, had been tight-locked with the enemy. She fought him in the true old-Navy fashion, which until this action it had seemed that modern conditions would prevent from ever being revived. Being second in line the *Broke* was uncovered to the rest of the enemy after the *Swift* marked down her opponent and sought to close with him. Captain E. R. G. R. Evans, C.B. (the well-known Antarctic explorer), who commanded the *Broke*, torpedoed the second enemy vessel.

H.M.S. *Swift*

Then he turned upon the Germans every one of the *Broke's* guns that could be made to bear. Six enemy destroyers were opposed to her. All of them were driving at full speed. Flames pouring out of their funnels showed the boats up with a weird distinctness that gave Captain Evans his chance to strike surely. And strike surely he did. Porting helm he drove the *Broke* head foremost at the third enemy vessel, crashing into her squarely just behind the after funnel.

With the *Broke's* razor-like bows embedded deeply in the German's hull the two vessels became fast clenched. A desperate hand-to-hand fight ensued. At point-blank range the *Broke* swept the German's decks with all possible guns. And she herself had to bear the brunt of a furious attack in return. Two German destroyers poured into her a destructive fire. Of the eighteen men working the *Broke's* foremost guns soon only six were left. These, headed by Midshipman Donald A. Gyles, R.N.R., who was wounded in the eye, kept these guns in action.

Now the crew of the destroyer with which the *Broke* was at hand-grips swarmed over the forecastle and tried to capture the *Broke* by boarding her. On they came, a shouting, frenzied mob, sweeping right past the muzzles of the forward guns, whose flashes blinded and confused them. Midshipman Gyles, though half blinded by blood, stood up to them single-handed, using an automatic pistol.

One German who threw himself upon Gyles and tried to wrench the pistol away from him was bayoneted by Able Seaman Ingleson. Furiously and fast waged the fight on the *Broke's* narrow decks, where dead and dying lay beneath the feet of the combatants. Using cutlasses, rifles, and bayonets, the survivors of the *Broke's* crew threw themselves at the boarding party, and a strenuous encounter ended in all the invaders being swept over the ship's side, save two who lay down and feigned death. These were taken prisoners.

Wrenching herself free from the enemy, which by now was in a sinking condition (it was the boat which the *Swift* saw go down later), the *Broke* made an unsuccessful attempt to attack

21

a second German. But though this failed the *Broke* hit another with a torpedo. Out of the six enemy destroyers two only were now left in action. The *Broke* attacked these. But a shell penetrating her boiler and disabling her main engine at this moment stopped her from hanging on to them, and they slipped away. The *Broke* proceeded towards an enemy vessel which was burning some little distance off.

Noticing the *Broke* coming, the crew of this craft began to call for mercy and shout loudly to be saved. The British Navy never turns a deaf ear to such an appeal from a beaten foeman. In response to it the *Broke* began limping painfully towards the burning ship with the intention of taking off the crew at whatever risk to herself.

But the Germans who had been thus clamouring for mercy suddenly opened fire upon the vessel that was coming to succour them. The *Broke's* reply to this mean act was four rounds from her own guns, followed by a torpedo that struck the foe amidships. Being unable to move out of his range the *Broke* had perforce to protect herself in this way against any further treachery on the part of the enemy. As a result of this brilliant engagement two, and probably three, enemy destroyers out of the flotilla of six were sunk. This flotilla had come from Zeebrugge with the intention of raiding British shipping in the Straits of

H.M.S. *Broke*

Dover when the *Swift* and the *Broke* fell upon them.

The lesson thus taught to the Hun was underlined and otherwise emphasized on March 22 of this year. Between 4 and 5 a.m. on that day the enemy's Zeebrugge flotilla was again caught by ships of the Dover Patrol and again suffered a heavy defeat. The flotilla had bombarded Dunkirk and was stealing homeward when a force of two British and three French destroyers led by H.M.S. *Botha* fell upon it.

Foggy weather prevailed at the time, and the Germans endeavoured by taking advantage of this to slip away without coming to an engagement. They did not want to fight. But the Allied force held them up and made them. As a consequence of the encounter four of the enemy craft were destroyed, whilst on our side the casualties were infinitesimal, only one destroyer being damaged.

So much the worse did he get of these and sundry other "scraps" that the Hun has persistently refused all challenges to open combat ever since. If his ships do venture out of the harbour they promptly bolt in again whenever danger threatens in the shape of our warships. Also, the enemy shows a distinct preference for cruising behind the shelter of his minefields to steaming in the open sea.

Although this cautious timidity limits their risks, it does not ensure absolute immunity from attack for his ships. Rarely does a day go by without some portion or other of the Dover Patrol hammering the Hun at some point along the Belgian coast.

Out from Dunkirk, with slow ungainly gait, trudges a batch of monitors, accompanied by motor-launches and other satellites for making smokescreens. At the chosen spot, which may be off Zeebrugge or Ostend, or where troublesome coastal batteries are known to be located—and all these receive due attention in turn—the smoke-makers start putting up their screens. From behind this cover the monitors train their big guns shoreward. Up go the muzzles to extreme elevation and the pounding begins. Aircraft are meanwhile directing the fall of the shot and incidentally themselves doing something towards worrying the

Hun.

Quite commonly he gets it three ways at once. Monitors shell him from the sea, aircraft bomb him from overhead, and siege-guns bombard him along the coast. The Hun does not take all this lying down. He has strewn the Belgian coast so full of big guns that they bristle up amongst the sand-dunes as thickly as prickles on a hedgehog's back. But whilst they are there they cannot be used against the Allies at any other place; neither can the men who man them, and that counts as a considerable military gain, especially as the Hun coastal artillery does scarcely any harm to our ships, although the latter knock out his batteries pretty frequently.

By pounding him over the coast-line in this manner during the earlier stages of the war the ships of the Dover Patrol helped materially to stop the enemy from reaching Calais. They are still preventing him from developing the stretch of Belgian coast-line which he holds into the formidable base for offensive operations against us which he had intended to make of it. Instead of attacking us from there he has been driven back upon the defensive and cannot get away with anything else.

Because of the position it holds, the operations of the Dover Patrol are of especial importance to the British public. One way or another it has played a prominent part in the war right from the beginning. More actual fighting has been done on this sector of the "sea front" than upon any.

Fighting of one sort or another occurs here almost daily; because this is the only stretch of salt water that the enemy can be reached from. To this extent the fortune of war favours the Dover Patrol, and makes its doings extremely interesting. But one should not take too circumscribed a view even of these. Sea matters, above any, need looking at in the right perspective and with a due sense of proportion. Viewing them thus comprehensively one recognizes at once the great outstanding fact that during the first two and a half years of war particularly, the British Navy protected the world at large from miseries indescribable by standing betwixt it and Germany.

When our Fleet closed the seas against Germany it sealed her doom and saved civilization. One must be content to merely state this truth here, and not demonstrate it at length. But the truth should be recognized, as it is an all-important one. And though the work of the Dover Patrol touches us all so nearly, readers should clearly understand that this unit of our splendid navy only fills its allotted place in the general scheme of national defence, as other units fill theirs. Britain's sea-power reaches long hands into practically every sea. And it is the greatest national asset our Empire possesses.

CHAPTER 3

Twisting the Dragon's Tail and What We Gained by it

Now we come to the story of one of the greatest feats of arms ever accomplished by a naval force, and it stands to the credit of the Dover Patrol. The sealing up of Zeebrugge on the night of April 23 takes rank with such imperishable achievements as the attack upon Cadiz. In fact, the singeing of the King of Spain's beard by Sir Francis Drake at Cadiz and the twisting of the dragon's tail by Sir Roger Keyes at Zeebrugge have features of similarity which place them in a class apart.

The success of the Zeebrugge operations was due as much to the excellence of the staff work which preceded it as to the bravery of the officers and men who carried the operation through. "Staff work" means organization, careful planning and the exercise of an astute prevision so that all emergencies may be provided against, and the element of chance eliminated as completely as possible. Long before our ships turned their bows with fighting intent towards the submarine and destroyer base which Germany had established at the mouth of the Bruges Canal the scheme of attack had been worked out to the minutest detail.

Every officer and man had been thoroughly rehearsed in the part given him to play. Nothing was left to the hazard of the moment. Everyone went into the enterprise knowing what he should do in any emergency that might arise. In so far as skilled generalship could assure such a result the expedition was won even before it was started. It is well that this aspect of the matter should be clearly understood; that in viewing the splendid success obtained one should not overlook the foundation on which it was built and which made that success possible.

The more one knows about the undertaking the clearer does the value of the preparatory work become. For the attack upon Zeebrugge, though carried through with sublime dash and courage in its last and most important stage, was not the outcome of a brilliant inspiration conceived on the impulse of the moment and put into execution as soon as thought of. On the contrary, the expedition had to wait long and anxiously for the opportune moment.

Twice the ships started towards their goal, twice they had to turn back again as conditions were unfavourable to the success of their enterprise. The minds which planned this had the fortitude to resist all temptations to a premature assault which might have imperilled success. And it was this unerring skill in choosing the right moment to strike, and refusing to strike otherwise than surely, which created the conditions that enabled Sir Roger Keyes' little squadron to inflict such a signal defeat on the enemy.

Like most other great schemes the plan of the Zeebrugge operation was quite simple in so far as its essential features were concerned. The main object sought was to block the mouth of the Bruges Canal. Everything else was subsidiary to this. For example, although the *Vindictive's* attack upon the Mole developed into such a wonderful feat of arms, it was, like the submarine's equally remarkable exploit in blowing up the viaduct, designed merely as a side-show in order to attract the attention of the enemy and thus enable the three blocking ships to arrive at their goal.

Zeebrugge being the point of entry for the Bruges Canal into the North Sea had long been a source of annoyance to us. The enemy had made of it a strong, well-equipped submarine and destroyer base from which he was able to make "tip-and-run" raids by means of surface craft, and to send out U-boats

Sir Roger Keyes

both for mine-laying and commerce-destroying purposes. The vessels he used for these purposes could lie in comfort and comparative safety in the outer harbour at Zeebrugge, where the Mole protected them from the bad weather and minefields to some extent protected them against the British Fleet.

Whenever our warships made a raid upon the place and shelled the outer harbour until it became untenable, as they frequently used to do, the whole of the enemy vessels would retire into the Bruges Canal, and thus get out of the reach of our longest range guns. In fact, the canal was a "funkhole" into which they could withdraw when danger threatened, and, likewise, a jumping-off point from which they could obtain a favourable start on raiding expeditions, particularly upon those short dashes on dark nights to which the German destroyer flotillas are addicted.

It was the Bruges Canal which enabled the enemy to turn Zeebrugge into the hornets' nest he made of it for us, and it was to block up this canal and make it of no further value to the enemy that our operations, carried through to success on April 23, were undertaken. As everyone knows, the expedition attained its objective with most important results for us, and most disastrous ones for the enemy.

One of the heaviest handicaps laid upon him during the war has been that our Fleet cut him off from access to the sea. The Ems, the Elbe, and the Baltic have been of little use to him, except for passing out submarines, in so far as reaching the wide waters is concerned. But once he got possession of the splendid canal system of Flanders he was able to open two gateways for his small craft into the North Sea at points most awkward for us—*viz*. Zeebrugge and Ostend.

Of the two the former was the most valuable to him because of the deep-water canal running straight betwixt it and Bruges. There is another canal connecting Bruges with Ostend, but this is so shallow that for transporting destroyers it is quite useless. As a result of our having placed two blocking ships in the mouth of the Bruges Canal, and subsequently, by means of our aircraft, sinking a German destroyer alongside them, the mouth of the Bruges Canal has been sealed up, at any rate for the duration of the war. Some dozen or more of the enemy's best destroyers and several of his large submarines are bottled up in the docks at Bruges, unable to reach the sea either by way of Zeebrugge or Ostend, and therefore useless to him. As a base from which sporadic raids can be made into the Straits of Dover or the North Sea, Zeebrugge has been robbed of most of its utility to the Germans.

Ostend is far less convenient to them for this purpose. For one thing it is nearer our Dover Patrol bases, and consequently more easily watched. Also, it lies within the range of our siege-guns ashore, whilst our ships shell it ceaselessly from the sea. Added to, this the channels within the port have been partly blocked by the *Vindictive*, which was sunk there on the night of May 9, so that as a base for raiding craft Ostend does not now hold many possibilities for the enemy.

What the virtual destruction of these two bases means to the people of the United Kingdom may be gathered from what has been said of their menace to all our sea-going traffic bound for the Port of London or other places in the North Sea. From the Belgian coast to the Downs the Thames Estuary is but a few hours' run for a fast destroyer of the type which the enemy used to operate from Ostend and Zeebrugge, and no merchant ship passing into the Thames could ever be sure when one of these sea-wolves would make a sudden pounce upon it.

As a result of the expedition we are describing, this danger has almost disappeared. It can never be absolutely eliminated, because the Germans have assembled a flotilla in the outer harbour of Zeebrugge, presumably in the hope that they will some time or another get a chance of using them. But the fact remains that whilst the ships that bring us food and carry out our merchandise pass to and fro right in face of him, he is powerless to do them hurt. And we owe this satisfactory state of affairs chiefly to the magnificent service done by the Dover Patrol in "bottling up" the enemy's sea bases in Flanders.

H.M.S. *VINDICTIVE AFTER THE RAID*

Official announcements of new "prohibited areas" made about the time the "bottling up" was successfully accomplished shows that this was only part of an extensive scheme for closing the North Sea. They were links in a wide-reaching chain forged for the purpose of fettering the enemy's naval movements. Unless this fact is continually remembered the importance of these operations cannot be correctly understood. There has been a barrage across the Straits of Dover for a long time. Now our navy has blocked the other end of the North Sea as well by laying a gigantic minefield there.

By translating into plain terms the official particulars as to latitude and longitude one gets the fact that the new "prohibited area" takes the form of a large triangle which encloses an area of approximately 122,000 square miles of water. Some 400 miles across, its base runs from the Scotch coast to the edge of the Norwegian three miles' limit.

On its longer sides the triangle measures 650 miles. Germany will doubtless send out her U-boats by way of Norwegian territorial waters since she is no respecter of neutrality. But owing to this stupendous "danger zone "having been created by our Fleet, her submarines must either take the great risk of passing through some hundreds of miles of mine-strewn sea, or else make a detour of 1300 miles towards the Arctic to get round the apex of the triangle. That means for them an extra 2600 miles of travelling out and home, with a resultant decrease by this distance of their radius of action once they reach their "hunting ground." And that helps the Allies' anti-submarine campaign tremendously.

With both exits from the North Sea closed against them, and their most troublesome "port of issue" into it blocked, U-boats will have an increasingly "lean" time.

The Fight Upon The Mole

The attack upon Zeebrugge was carried out under the direction of Vice-Admiral Sir Roger Keyes, K.C.B., in command of the Dover Patrol, who flew his flag in the destroyer *Warwick*. Counting all in there were somewhere about seventy ships of various sorts engaged in the operation. These included the motor-launches which made the smokescreens, the monitors which carried out a long-range bombardment, the coastal motor-boats which operated inshore, and the destroyers which, as it were, kept the ring for the central combat and looked for a force of enemy destroyers that were known to be at sea.

But the latter exercised the better part of valour by keeping well out of the way. For blocking up the entrance of the Bruges Canal three old warships, *Thetis, Intrepid*, and *Iphigenia*, had been filled with concrete and fitted with explosive bombs which would sink them immediately fuses were blown. The old cruiser *Vindictive* had been specially fitted and detailed to make an attack upon the Mole whilst an obsolete submarine loaded with explosives was ordered to blow up the viaduct connecting the Mole with the shore.

Twice before had the expedition sailed, but weather conditions necessitated a postponement of the operation. On this occasion, however, the elements were sufficiently favourable to enable the attack to be carried through. At a certain point the force fell into their fighting formation and proceeded towards their objective. The night was dark and there was a rather heavy

In the foretop of the *Vindictive* - Men of the Royal Marine Artillery fought here with pom-poms and Lewis guns. It was struck by a shell.

sea running, which made matters difficult for some of the smaller craft and considerably handicapped the party which stormed the Mole.

The *Vindictive*, the blocking-ships, and the submarine were manned only by volunteers as it was deemed very unlikely that anyone would survive. And it says much for the spirit of the British Navy that although to be in the van of this expedition was generally regarded as going to certain death, there were many times more than the required number of officers and men who volunteered for it. The authorities were overwhelmed with offers of service.

"Everybody wanted to go, and our great difficulty was in sorting out those we required from the huge number of volunteers," said the First Sea Lord, when explaining the basis upon which the expedition was formed and the necessity for having in it only those who were so accustomed to acting together that there could be no possible chance of any confusion arising during the intensive hand-to-hand fighting which it was known would occur amidst the smoke and darkness. So keen were the men that when it was proposed to lessen the complement of one of the ships those "weeded out" flatly refused to leave her.

An essential feature in ensuring success was that the ships should be well screened by clouds of artificial fog. The work of creating this was entrusted to the motor- launches under command of Captain R. Collins, R.N. These fell into their assigned positions and started their smoke going so skilfully that the main expedition was enabled to approach under cover of it and to get to fairly close quarters before the enemy were aware of their coming.

Everything worked perfectly as planned. The blocking-ships made straight for harbour, the submarine took her course towards the viaduct, whilst the *Vindictive* headed for the Mole. For the purposes of narrative, what then happened may be divided into three sections: the *Vindictive's* assault on the Mole, the sinking of the blocking-ships, and the blowing up of the submarine. Each of these is an immortal story.

Let us take the *Vindictive* first. With dense smokescreens rolling before, she headed straight for the Mole, aiming to lay herself alongside the batteries upon it and close to the seaplane sheds which it contained, and which it was part of the *Vindictive's* duty to demolish. "St. George for England" (it was St. George's Bay), signalled Sir Roger Keyes to her. "May we give the Dragon's tail a damned good twist," replied the *Vindictive*, and unquestionably she did this.

The Mole is a mile long and eighty yards wide. To facilitate landing her storming force the *Vindictive* had been fitted along one side with a high false deck, upon which were some nineteen brows, or gangways, for landing purposes. These were triced up in readiness to be dropped on the Mole immediately the *Vindictive* scraped alongside it. Many ancient devices have been revived during the war. This was one.

For the brows dropped by the *Vindictive* had their counterpart ages ago in the boarding gangway that used to be thrown out from Roman war-galleys. Accompanying her were the *Iris* and the *Daffodil*, two ex-Liverpool ferryboats. Midnight was chosen for the attack to begin. As the *Vindictive* got close in to the Mole the wind shifted, and blowing away the smokescreens that had enveloped the ship showed her clearly to the Germans. Promptly these gave the alarm by firing star-shells, and very soon the sky was alight with these, whilst searchlights were sweeping about endeavouring to penetrate the fog. The star-shells amid the smoke burst with a curious ghastly green glare, weird and unearthly.

As soon as the oncoming ship was revealed to them the Germans turned upon her every weapon they could bring to bear. The shelling soon rose to a perfect hurricane, pom-pom, machine-guns, and large-calibre artillery pouring projectiles into her as rapidly as they could. In the face of this deadly onslaught she was navigated with the utmost coolness and skill. When she ran alongside the Mole, which was thirty feet high, and towered well above her decks, the sea beat her up and down against the wall of it so heavily that as her landing brows were dropped they

BIRD'S-EYE VIEW OF THE SUCESSFUL BRITISH RAID UPON THE
GERMAN SUBMARINE BASE AT ZEEBRUGGE NOTE THE POSITION OF
BLOCKING CRUISERS AND HOW THE *DAFFODIL* HELD THE
VINDICTIVE AGAINST THE MOLE

were nearly all smashed up and rendered useless. But she went into position as easily as a liner berthing beside a jetty, and then signalled to the *Daffodil* to give her a push in. The band of heroes who manned her at once swarmed over her sides and on to the Mole in any way they could, sweeping down like a human typhoon upon the enemy force stationed there. They had come through an inferno themselves to make an even worse one for the enemy.

"On emerging from the smokescreen," says Captain A. T. B. Carpenter, V.C., who commanded the *Vindictive*, describing her experiences, "the end of the Mole where the lighthouse stands was seen to be about 400 yards ahead of us. We immediately turned our ship towards the Mole, and increased to full speed so as to get alongside as soon as possible. It was our plan not to open fire until the enemy began to fire on us, as in that way we hoped to remain unobserved till the last possible moment.

When the enemy began firing at us we were only about 300 yards away from the muzzles of his guns. We at once replied with every weapon aboard the *Vindictive* that could be brought to bear on the foe, and we fired at him as hard as we could. After nearly five minutes of this the *Vindictive* slid into position by the Mole, which we endeavoured to grapple so as to keep her in place. This proved difficult, and one of our grapplings tore away a great lump of concrete from the Mole, which fell aboard the ship, and we brought it away with us when we returned.

The *Daffodil*, which was following close to our stern, came up, and putting her bows against the *Vindictive*, pushed the latter vessel sideways until she got close to the Mole. There the *Daffodil* helped to hold her by pressing her bows against the *Vindictive's* side so that the latter ship could not drift away. Owing to the heavy swell which was on, the work of securing the Mole proved very difficult. When the brows were run out from the *Vindictive* the men at once climbed along them.

It was an extremely perilous thing to do in view of the fact that at one moment the ends of the brows were from eight to ten feet above the wall, and at the next moment were crashing on the wall itself as the ship rolled up and down. The way in which the men got over those brows seemed almost superhuman. I expected every moment to see them falling off between the Mole and the ship, a drop of at least thirty feet, and being crushed by the ship against the wall. But not a man fell; their agility was wonderful.

It was not a case of a seaman running barefoot along the deck of a rolling ship. The men as they landed were carrying heavy accoutrements, such as bombs, Lewis guns, and other articles, but they never hesitated. They went along the brows on to the Mole at the utmost possible speed. Within a few minutes three or four hundred of them had landed, and under cover of a barrage put down on the Mole by Stokes guns and howitzer fire they fought their way along the top. Comparatively few of the German guns were able to hit the hull of our ship as it was behind the protection of the wall. In fact, safety depended on how near we could get to the enemy guns instead of upon how far we could get away from them.

Whilst the hull was thus guarded, the upper works of the *Vindictive*, that is, funnels, masts, ventilators and so forth, which showed above the wall, were made a target upon which a large number of German guns concentrated. Many of our casualties were caused by splinters coming down from the upper part of the ship, and if it had not been for the *Daffodil* continuing to push her in towards the wall all the time fighting was in progress, none of the men who went on the Mole would have got back again.

After we had been alongside about twenty-five minutes we saw the blocking-ships rounding the lighthouse and making for the canal entrance. And then we knew that our work had been successfully accomplished. Just before this the submarine had been blown up under the viaduct, and the cheer raised by my men in the *Vindictive* when they saw the terrific explosion was one of the finest things I ever heard. Many of the men were severely wounded, some had been hit three or four times, but they had no thought except for the success of the operation."

Part of the *Vindictive's* fighting complement was composed of the 4th Royal Marine Battalion, commanded by Colonel Bertram Nowell Elliot, D.S.O. The bluejacket landing party was under Captain Henry Crosby Halahan, D.S.O., R.N. Neither of these officers was fated to lead ashore the men he had so carefully trained for fighting there. The men were assembled on the main deck and the lower deck ready at the given signal to rush up the broad sloping ways which led to the false deck from where the brows were thrown out. These decks being below the level of the wall the men on them were fairly well sheltered until they got the order to advance.

Colonel Elliot and Captain Halahan, both of whom occupied an exposed position on the false deck, were killed as the *Vindictive* hove alongside. Captain Halahan was caught by machine-gun bullets, whilst Colonel Elliot was struck by a shell which caused a great many fatalities in the forward Stokes mortar battery. In addition to being specially equipped for throwing men ashore, the *Vindictive* had been specially armed for fighting at close quarters.

Distributed about various parts of her decks were little sandbagged emplacements for Stokes mortar and machine guns, and she had a similarly protected howitzer fore and aft. From these positions a deadly fire was directed upon the enemy for as long as the weapons situated in them could be used, and particularly whilst the storming parties were scrambling on the Mole.

As soon as these received the word to go they swept forward and poured in a rapid stream over the couple of brows which the rolling of the ship alongside the wall had left intact. From the swaying ends of these the men leaped into a stream of machine-gun bullets, and many of them became casualties.

One of the first to fall was Commander Brock, R.N.A.S., who perfected the smokescreen appliances. Yet the advance never once wavered or slackened. Lieutenant H. T. C. Walker, whilst leading the men towards the Mole, had one of his arms carried away by a shell. He fell, and in the darkness (for except for the fitful gleams from the muzzles of discharging guns and the eerie light of bursting star-shells it was very dark) the hurrying feet of the stormers passed over him until he was seen by another officer, who dragged him aside. Thereupon Lieutenant Walker, raising himself, waved his remaining arm and shouted words of encouragement to the attacking party as they rushed past him.

On the Mole the scene was indescribable. As our men advanced so they threw bombs, used bludgeons, cutlasses, axes, rifles, bayonets, in a hand-to-hand *mêlée* which the enemy did not very long face. Whilst he could use his guns from behind a fairly safe shelter he stuck bravely to his post, but the fierce onslaught of shouting men, armed with various weapons and all intent upon coming to handgrips with the foe, which was hurled at him from the *Vindictive*, in the end sent the enemy scuttling to cover wherever he could find it.

But amidst all the mad excitement of the fray, and though the fighting spirit was strong upon them, our men did not forget the work for which they had been trained. Each party as it landed upon the Mole made straight for the definite objective assigned to it. Some ran to the seaplane sheds and demolished them, some made a direct attack upon certain batteries, others used bombs with most destructive effect upon some German destroyers lying just inside the Mole, and which had been lobbing projectiles over it at the *Vindictive*.

The work of clearing the Mole was most effectively done, the enemy being driven shoreward, covering himself with machine-guns as he fell back. Whilst they were thus employed amidst burning buildings, dynamite rent emplacements, clouds of rolling smoke with great gusts of machine-gun fire sweeping through them; amidst surroundings so weird that they seemed like a dream to those who passed safely through them, our men could see the blocking-ships force their way into the canal mouth and encouraged them with a hearty cheer. For an hour this sort of thing went on.

CHAPTER 4

Through the Jaws of Hell

But the *Vindictive* did something more than bring the storming party alongside and put them into enemy territory. During the whole of the time the fight lasted she took an active part in it. Whilst she lay by the Mole her guns continued firing, and she threw out broad sheets of liquid fire from the flame-throwing cabin built just forward of her bridge. It was in this cabin, a very exposed situation, forming as it did a target which the enemy guns could not miss, that Captain Carpenter stood when taking his vessel into her berth. In a very short time the cabin was literally blown to pieces. The captain had the peak of his cap shot away, and several bullet-holes through his clothes, but escaped with a comparatively slight wound. Not so fortunate were those nearby him.

A huge shell came rattling over the parapet and struck the *Vindictive* just by her bridge, pounding the chart-room there into a mass of jumbled wreckage. Towering just above this was her fighting-top, which was manned by a party of Royal Marine Artillery under command of Lieutenant C. N. B. Rigby, R.M.A. The outside of the top was stoutly protected by splinter mats, and from inside it the Marine gunners poured a deadly stream of pom-pom and machine-gun bullets into the enemy as long as they could fight at all.

But the prominent position of the top, standing high above the wall of the Mole, made it a distinctive mark for the enemy's artillery, which turned their full strength upon it in order to silence the guns that were punishing them so heavily. Lieutenant Rigby was killed, and all the others in the top were either killed outright or became bad casualties, save only Sergeant Finch. Shot down and wounded, Finch struggled from beneath a heap of dead and dying comrades. He then grasped the handle of a pom-pom and kept this in action right until the last.

The fighting-top was naught but a small circular steel chamber in which men were cramped elbow to elbow. By the time the *Vindictive* drew off it was piled with dead and dying; the wreckage of knocked-out guns and other pitiful debris of a hard-won fight. Other parts of the ship also suffered heavily. Shells ploughed their way through the raised wooden deck and burst below. One killed or wounded practically a whole howitzer's crew.

A second crew promptly took the gun, but were swept down by shellfire, whereupon a third crew took their places at the weapon. The *Vindictive's* funnels were torn absolutely to ribbons. Hundreds of projectiles must have gone through them, for the outer casings hung in tatters from the deck level to their tops. The decks themselves were knee-deep in wreckage of all sorts. Dead and wounded men lay all about them, and they were almost impassable with blood-stained garments that had been cast aside, weapons hastily thrown down or dropped by failing hands, empty shell-cases, belts of ammunition, and the hundred and one other litters that accumulate during a fight.

When her work was done and she was ready to withdraw, the *Vindictive*, by means of her syren, gave the recall signal to those who had landed from her. But the din of the fighting was so tremendous that the signal could not be heard. Therefore it was repeated and repeated many times. Every effort to re-embark men was made, and the ship did not cast off from the Mole until assured that everybody who could possibly do so had got aboard her. Now occurred one of those instances of self-sacrificing heroism that are so frequent in the annals of our warfare, be it by land or sea.

Captain Palmer, who was in charge of the Marines landed

on the Mole, refused to rejoin the *Vindictive* because he could not muster all his men and take them back with him. "Come aboard; all are on but you, and we are just going to shove off," he was told.

"No, I can't find all my men, and I am not coming away without them," replied the captain, and on the Mole he stayed. It is understood that he was taken prisoner, and was subsequently interviewed by the Kaiser when the All-Highest hurried down to Zeebrugge next day to personally investigate what damage the British expedition had done there.

The fortunes of the *Daffodil* and the *Iris* were so closely allied to those of the *Vindictive* that all may be considered as constituting one episode of the fight. It had been intended that after the *Daffodil* had helped to berth the *Vindictive* she should go alongside the Mole and land her own men upon it. But her services were required, as before explained, to hold the *Vindictive* in position. A strenuous task and magnificently performed.

In doing it the *Daffodil*'s engines had to be worked up to just double their normal pressure of steam per square inch and kept at that. Being sheltered by the larger ship, the *Daffodil* suffered but few casualties. Lieutenant H. Campbell, her commanding officer, was wounded by a shell splinter, one of her men was killed, and seven of them injured.

Very much less fortunate than this was the *Iris*. She moved ahead of the *Vindictive* and tried to make fast to the Mole, but failed to do so as her grapnels were not large enough to span the parapet. Thereupon two of her officers, Lieutenant-Commander Bradford and Lieutenant Hawkins, climbed up on the parapet and sat astride it trying to make the grapnel hold fast. They continued doing this until both were killed and fell in the water between the ship and the wall.

Commander Valentine Gibbs, who commanded the *Iris*, had both his legs shot away by a shell which wrecked one end of her bridge, and he died next morning. With the commander out of action, Lieutenant Spencer, R.N.R. took charge of the ship, although he was wounded, and refused to be relieved. Eventually

MEMBERS OF THE CREW OF THE *VINDICTIVE*

the *Iris* was forced to change her position and come astern of the *Vindictive*. She was subjected to a devastating fire from which she suffered very heavily. One shell plunged through her upper deck and exploded in the midst of a party of marines who were waiting to go up the gangway. There were fifty-six men in this party; forty-nine of them were killed outright and the remaining seven wounded. Another shell found its way into the wardroom which was being used as a casualty dressing-station, and bursting there killed four officers and twenty-six men. The *Iris*, in short, was reduced to little better than a shambles in a very brief time by a succession of heavy shells which plunged into her. By great good luck none of these damaged her engines or holed her beneath the water-line.

When the ships drew away from the Mole they exposed themselves to further attack from a heavy enemy battery which had been unable to reach them whilst they were masked by the wall. This promptly opened fire upon them and threw salvo after salvo in their direction, but all three of the vessels were making their best possible speed. The *Vindictive's* engines worked up to as many revolutions as they had done in her best steaming days. Consequently the enemy's shell mostly fell short.

Just when the Germans were getting the range effectively the *Vindictive* and her two consorts disappeared into the clouds of smoke which the motor-boats were making, and which in all probability saved the ships from being sunk by the enemy's long-range batteries. As it was they did not get off without further injury. The *Vindictive's* coxswain was killed at his post, whereupon Captain Carpenter took the wheel himself and steered out of action the ship he had so gallantly taken into it.

How splendid was the spirit of the *Vindictive's* men was illustrated by the reception given her captain when he made the round of the decks on the way home. As Captain Carpenter passed amongst them, even the badly wounded raised themselves up to cheer him. "Have we won?" was their eager query. So long as the enemy had been defeated nothing else mattered.

CHAPTER 6

A Submarine's Immortal Exploit

Next in point of time to the *Vindictive's* attack upon the Mole came the destruction by a submarine of the viaduct which connected the Mole with the shore. This viaduct was constructed of open piling with oak planking and iron gratings on the top of it. At the lower end of the Mole, where the viaduct joined it, were the sheds of a sea-plane base, concrete shelters for men, and other buildings. The S.S. *Brussels*, Captain Fryatt's old ship, which the Germans used as a torpedo training-school, lay on the inside of the Mole just under the seaplane hangars, and there was a shelter for submarines a little higher up.

The *Vindictive* berthed alongside the Mole at the point where that structure bends around towards the lighthouse, situated at the extreme end of it. Her objective was to distract the enemy's attention so that the blocking-ships, when they arrived a little later, would be able to pass the lighthouse unnoticed by the Germans; or, at least, would find the latter so much occupation that they could not concentrate all their strength upon checking the blocking-ships' progress.

Similarly, the purpose of the submarine's attack upon the viaduct was to breach it, and thus prevent reinforcements being rushed from the shore along the Mole in support of the enemy, who were having such a rough time at the hands of the *Vindictive's* storming party. How she performed the exceptionally dangerous task allotted her constitutes one of the bravest of the many brave deeds that sparkle like priceless gems in the golden

47

setting of our naval history. Really there exists no parallel to this wonderful exploit, as nothing like it had ever been done before.

From start to finish it was as full of peril as anything well could be. So much so that nobody, not even themselves, expected that the small volunteer crew which manned her would come safely through their great adventure. The odds against them appeared so overwhelming that, even if they succeeded, in doing the thing assigned them it was deemed a certainty that their lives would pay the penalty of their achievement. One must grasp this fact and all it conveys before one can rightly appraise the magnificent quality of the courage shown by this little band of half a dozen stout-hearted seamen.

The submarine chosen for the work was a boat of obsolete type. By way of preparation for the occasion she had been stuffed full of high explosive, several tons of it, until the devastating capacity of her cargo equalled in destructive force the power of some forty-odd German submarine mines. That of itself will give some idea of what she held embowelled within her, and illustrate dangers which beset her crew; as well as the difficulties they had to face whilst getting the boat to her destination. For them it was peril all the way.

Before they were put to the supreme test of blowing up their boat and, as was believed would happen, themselves with her, they had to navigate the submarine for about one hundred miles through a rough sea. From her home base until Zeebrugge was reached she had to be towed by a destroyer. Going under her own power in the circumstances was out of the question. Towing her proved an awkward enough task. During the whole of this hundred miles her crew were sitting atop of what was actually a huge mine, heavily loaded, with the waves breaking over them continually. Much trouble was experienced in steering the submarine, and there was an ever-present risk that the towline would part and leave her drifting helplessly at the mercy of heavy seas.

One gets a fairly realistic glimpse of what her complement

had to withstand on their way across the North Sea from the experiences of a picket-boat that accompanied them. This picket-boat had been detailed to attend upon the submarine after Zeebrugge was reached.

Amongst other things the intention was that the boat should escort her towards the viaduct, putting up on the way a smoke-screen, under shelter of which she could approach her objective unseen. Also, that the boat should do its best to rescue her complement after they had blown up their vessel. But no matter how carefully an operation may be planned, arrangements can seldom be carried through in their entirety where the vagaries of the weather, as well as the uncertainties of war, are both influencing factors. It turned out so in this instance. The picket-boat also had to be towed. And owing to the heavy swell and other adverse weather conditions the boat towed very badly.

Several times she almost turned over until, finally, only the breaking up of the tow-line at a critical moment saved her from capsizing altogether. As a result of this she fell behind the submarine, which had to go along without her. In the end this proved a fortunate accident, as if the picket-boat had remained in company with her, the wholly unforeseen circumstance which enabled the submarine to succeed in her mission could hardly have arisen.

At a point four miles distant from the Mole the submarine began moving under her own power. From this period until she was rent into innumerable fragments there was not a single moment in her progress but held its gripping thrill. The boat was under command of Lieutenant R. D. Sandford, R.N., who had with him Lieutenant Price, R.N.R., Able Seaman Hamer (coxswain), Leading Torpedoman Cleaver, Chief E.R.A. Roxburgh, and Stoker Bendall. Like every other feature of the operations, the manner in which the submarine's part in them should be carried through had been carefully mapped out beforehand in the fullest possible detail. In so far as foresight could ensure this nothing was left to chance, though the god of chance dipped in his oar all the same.

The picket-boat having perforce been left behind, a smoke-screen was made for the submarine by other craft. Behind this cover she crept until within two miles of the viaduct, where she turned and made for it. Then occurred a thing that seemed at first certain to seal her doom, and probably would have done so if an even more remarkable event had not happened immediately upon the heels of it. A sudden shift of the wind uncloaked her by blowing the smokescreen the wrong way, so that instead of enveloping the vessel, the smoke left her exposed to the full view of the enemy. Star-shells were now lighting the water brilliantly, and searchlights pointing their broad white fingers about its surface in every direction.

Full in the glare of this eerie illumination, which threw her into much the same prominence as a dark object crossing a white screen, the submarine steered towards her goal. On the shore, just by the viaduct, were some nineteen heavy enemy guns. These started blazing at her furiously, beginning when she was 1500 yards away and shortening range until she had got within 500 yards of them. At the same time a large body of enemy riflemen stationed on the viaduct poured heavy volleys into her. Escape for boat or crew seemed impossible.

But although she formed such a prominent target, by extraordinary good luck neither boat nor any one in her was hit. Though incredibly fortunate in this respect, one may easily conceive what a tense period this was for the small band of heroes in charge of the boat and how heavily the strain of the situation must have tugged at their nerves. Remember, they were perched out on the top of a hollow steel cylinder filled with the most powerful of high explosives. Had a projectile struck the craft her risky cargo would have "gone off," and those piloting it along been blown into atoms within sight of their goal, with their task unfinished.

And they knew this fate might be theirs at any moment. Real acid of circumstance, a situation like this, to test what metal men are made of.

For about ten minutes the submarine proceeded, marvellously unscathed, through this deluge of steel and lead, with projectiles of various sizes beating up the water in angry spurts all round her. Then suddenly the firing stopped. Hellish pandemonium was followed by comparatively a dead silence—a strange and unexpected change, as surprising as it was at first difficult to account for. One divined the reason for it by what one saw on the viaduct.

Under the vivid constellation of star-shells the Huns, with which this structure was crowded, could be seen talking excitedly to each other, laughing and gesticulating. Apparently they were under the delusion that she had lost her course whilst seeking to enter the harbour, and was now groping blindly along the outside of the Mole trying to discover some way of repairing her error by getting through it and attacking the shipping inside. As to what she really aimed at obviously they had not the slightest inkling.

Seeing her making for the viaduct the Huns assumed that she meant trying to pass through the piling which supported it. "When she attempts that she will stick fast, then we can run down the ladders and capture boat and crew too," they told each other, congratulating themselves upon the ease with which they would secure the lot. And it was because they felt so sure of picking her up as a gift in this way that they left off firing at her. Little did the Huns know what the apparently lost sheep would do to them.

Their mistake afforded the submarine just the opportunity her crew were seeking. When about half a mile distant from the viaduct they got a clear view of it and of the point they were to strike. Turning the boat's head on towards this Lieutenant Sandford steered her direct for the place, the situation of which he knew, as where she should hit to attain her objective most effectively had been arranged beforehand. After a rapid survey of the position, Lieutenant Sandford determined to make sure at all costs and to avoid anything that involved the slightest risk of failure.

At full speed he drove the submarine straight at the viaduct, into the understructure of which she crashed, burying her fore-part in the timbers to a depth of forty feet, until her conning-tower came flat against the piling and thus brought her to a standstill. At this moment no man aboard her gave a thought to anything beyond the work in hand, though it seemed less likely than ever that any would survive the completion of it. The Huns who had been watching the approach of the submarine now started clambering down the ladders, all gleefully eager to seize the boat and her crew.

But the big surprise was on the point of being sprung upon the enemy. Having got their craft just where they wanted to place her—she was put under the viaduct at exactly the prear-ranged spot—Lieutenant Sandford and his comrades hastened their task. After starting the fuses they lowered a small dinghy which they carried for the purpose, clambered into it, and began to pull away when quite assured that the fuses would do their part effectively.

So that her crew might have a chance of getting clear quickly a powerful motor had been fitted in the dinghy supplied to the submarine. This motor was so much too powerful for the tiny boat that when running it shook her seams open. Consequently, a strong motor-pump was also placed in her. And to this fortui-tous circumstance the complement of the submarine owe their lives. After they jumped into the dinghy and started the motor, they found this to be useless for propulsion as the screw had fouled something and broken off when the dinghy was being dropped into the water. No other course was left them but to get out the oars, and they did so.

Heavy fire now assailed them again from the viaduct. The enemy, seeing their attempt to escape, gave vent to angry cries and renewed their rifle volleys, supplementing these by streams of bullets from machine-guns and pom-poms, being fully deter-mined that the crew should not get away. But the crew were of another mind. Determined to escape if they in any way could, they fought heroically for liberty in the face of most adverse conditions. Overweighted as she was with machinery, their dinghy at best would have pulled very sluggishly. Added to other handicaps a strong current kept sweeping them back towards the viaduct almost as rapidly as they rowed away from it—and they struggled desperately to put as much distance between themselves and it as possible, for they knew the danger of what was about to happen, if the enemy did not.

Very soon their boat became riddled with pom-pom bullets and made water so fast that she would have sunk and drowned all her occupants if the motor-pump had not been set going. This kept the inrushing water low enough for the dinghy to remain afloat. Still the bullets rained upon her. First, Lieutenant Sandford fell with a wound in his thigh and one hand smashed. Next Hamer, the coxswain, and Stoker Bendall were shot down. The three unwounded men plied the oars as vigorously as they could, but matters were looking very grave for them when the submarine went up with an appalling roar.

At the moment of the explosion the dinghy was only about two hundred yards from her, and onlookers thought that the tiny boat and its occupants must surely be "whiffed into nothingness" by the force of the terrific upheaval. Great was the relief when the tumbling water subsided and they were seen amidst the smoke still bending sturdily to their oars. But by the shock all gunfire had been checked for the time being and the enemy had suffered severely. As the fuses ignited the submarine's cargo there occurred one of the greatest explosions ever known on the sea.

A gap 120 feet wide was made in the viaduct, everything in this space being cut away cleanly, from water-line upwards, whilst some hundreds of the enemy who had swarmed on top of the structure in their haste to seize the submarine were blown away—and only portions of them came back again. Little bits of Hun, pieces of woodwork, and other fragments continued dropping into the water for some time afterwards, and over a considerable area.

Along the Mole searchlights were extinguished, their lenses splintering under the shock, whilst machine-guns were put out of action and the crews of heavier enemy artillery some distance away so badly stunned that for a time they could not go on firing.

The picket-boat in charge of Commander F. H. Sandford, D.S.O., R.N. (Lieutenant R. D. Sandford's brother), which had been told off to attend upon the submarine, now came up, having made a short cut to the scene of operations after her touring mishap. She picked up the submarine's complement and placed them aboard the destroyer *Phoebe*, where medical attention was given to the wounded amongst them.

Having done this the picket-boat, down by the head and so full of water that towing her would have been dangerous, made a risky voyage back to Dover under her own steam.

CHAPTER 7

How the Bruges Canal was Bottled up

After separating into three sections the units of the expedition that were designed to press close home upon the enemy each took its prescribed course towards a chosen goal. Much depended upon the timetable of movements being adhered to. This was kept with an accuracy that indicated a high standard of seamanship on the part of those who handled the ships.

Last to show themselves to the enemy was the trio of blocking-vessels. This consisted of the old cruisers *Thetis, Intrepid*, and *Iphigenia*, all of which had been filled with concrete so that once sunk in the fairway they would form a wall of steel and cement solidified across the mouth of the Bruges Canal. It had been planned to sink them close by the lock gates. To put them there was the main object of the expedition.

In the result this was so nearly attained as to make the operations a thorough success, although the ships did not quite reach the point where, as originally designed, they should have been blown up.

After the attack upon the Mole had been in progress some little time, long enough to absorb the enemy's attention and get him thoroughly busy in one particular direction, the main operation was developed. Swathed in clouds of smoke the three old cruisers steamed up to the harbour entrance. As they rounded the end of the Mole the star-shells and searchlights threw them into vivid relief before the eyes of a startled enemy, who, having no knowledge of what was really intended, probably thought the whole British Fleet had swooped upon him in a determined attempt to smash up his base for good and all. The very weight of the assault suggested strong forces behind it. Out of the darkness which hung over the sea, beyond the area lit up by the star-shells and searchlights, came the unnerving shriek of the big shells thrown in by the monitors that could not be seen and consequently their type and numbers only guessed at.

Projectiles fell from them in the manner of steady, persistent hammer-blows upon his shore defences, which were at the same time bombarded vigorously by our large guns planted on the coast-line and manned by the Royal Marine Artillery. Whilst they steamed in the blocking-ships plied their guns full blast also; thus adding to the enemy's uncertainty of mind—and to the deafening noise of the fray.

Battle pictures are difficult to draw, either in words or pencil. Whilst some idea of the action may be conveyed, the atmosphere amidst which it occurred, particularly the bewildering effects of the changing lights and awe-inspiring noises, cannot be recreated. And the mind that has never received a direct impression of such things is unable to visualize them accurately enough to do the picture justice. "It seemed as though the skies had broken up; that night was falling upon us in overwhelming wrath, and the mouth of Hades lay right beneath our bows," is how one member of the expedition described his impression of the scene around them as the blocking-ships fought their way into the harbour.

The *Thetis* led the van. Immediately she hove in sight, enemy guns from shore and sea opened a thunderous attack upon her. In addition to his batteries on the Mole, the enemy had many heavy guns upon the beach. These ran from Blankenberge, on the southward, right across the shore-line on either side of the canal, having been laid in position to beat off just such another attack as the one now being delivered. And the enemy gave our forces the full benefit of his batteries—machine-guns and pom-poms as well, for there were many of both studded in amongst the larger pieces. Only a skeleton crew was left aboard the *Thetis*, just sufficient to manoeuvre her into position and settle her there. The remainder of her men had been taken into safety aboard a motor-launch, according to programme.

But, mere navigating party though they were, those left in the *Thetis* kept her four guns in brisk action, as well as worked the ship. Out from the end of the Mole was strung a row of armed barges placed there for protection of the channel. The *Thetis* dodged clear of these, but had the bad luck to pick up on her screw the net defence stretched on the side of the barges. As her propeller turned quickly round it gathered these nets in a thick bunch about it. From that moment the *Thetis* became unmanageable owing to her screw being "seized up." Steer straight she would not, but reeled about as the currents swung her. However, she had torn a clear passage through the boom for the other two ships.

As the *Thetis* commenced to yaw about, the shore batteries picked her up and subjected her to a severe hammering, whilst she fought strenuously back. Struggling onwards, determined to reach the canal if possible, the *Thetis* stuck upon a bank, lurched off it again and got back into the channel. By this time the ship was in a sinking condition, so viciously had she been punished, and it became apparent that her end lay near. Yet she fought with unwavering courage, and as she lay shell-torn and derelict continued signalling to the *Intrepid* and *Iphigenia* information that proved of the greatest value in enabling them to make a safe advance towards their objective.

When the *Thetis* had struggled along until she almost reached the timber breakwater just outside the canal mouth, Commander R. S. Sneyd, D.S.O., R.N., in command of her, blew the charges which tore the final gaps in her now rapidly settling hull, and down she went in a slantwise position, partly across the channel that gives access to the canal. Though the *Thetis* did not succeed in entering the canal mouth, she was sunk in a position where she helps to most effectually bottle up this waterway. Of her small crew five were killed and five wounded. After the ship went down a motor-launch commanded by Lieutenant H. Littleton, R.N.V.R., made its way to the *Thetis* through the gale of shelling that still beat fiercely upon her and took off all survivors.

Whilst the *Thetis* thus went gallantly to the sacrifice, along came the *Intrepid*—abundantly justifying her name—with all guns blazing defiantly and dense volumes of camouflaging smoke rolling from her decks. A fearsome object indeed, she must have seemed to the Hun as she bore down aggressively upon him. In the shuddering confusion along the dark edges of the fight the launch which should have taken off the surplus of the *Intrepid's* crew was unable to reach her at the psychological moment, much to the satisfaction of the men thus left aboard the ship.

None of them had wanted to go from her whilst a fight lay ahead. Indeed, some who, regarded as supernumeraries, were ordered to be left behind, told their captain point-blank that they would not go out of the ship until the fight was over, and the captain, being an understanding man with all a sailor's large sympathy for a comrade who wants to get at the enemy, saw not the insubordinate side of their conduct in looking at the greater one and permitted them to stay. Through this, and the launch's inability to heave alongside, the *Intrepid* found herself so well manned that she had men enough for all purposes. And she made good use of them.

Straight towards the land she swept, guns roaring, crew cheering, smoke welling out of her in dense volume until she got a long way past the shore-line and some distance inside the mouth of the canal. There Lieutenant Stuart Bonham-Carter, R.N., the *Intrepid's* commanding officer, put the nose of his ship neatly upon the end of the western bank and let her swing across the canal.

Whilst this was happening her crew were removed in a motor-launch. When all was in readiness for abandoning ship, Lieutenant Bonham-Carter went into the chart-room and pulled the switches which fired the explosive charges in the vessel's interior. Four dull thuds were heard and at once the *Intrepid* began to seat herself firmly on the bottom. Unexpected testimony to the success of the explosion was supplied by the engineer officer, who had not left the engine-room when the fuses were blown, but came leaping up immediately afterwards with the report that all had gone well.

All this happened almost within hand-reach of the enemy on shore and plump against the muzzles of his guns. So close inshore that one officer escaped from the ship by jumping to the beach and running along the bank towards one of our launches that had crept in there. Whilst the officer ran, the enemy pelted him with machine-gun bullets, wounding him in the leg; as he jumped aboard the launch one of its crew attacked him with a hammer, mistaking him for a Hun.

Equally thrilling was the experience of Lieutenant Bonham-Carter. All the boats had pulled off before he was ready to leave the ship. Consequently he launched a float and jumped into the water with it. But instantly the float (a kind of big lifebuoy) touched the water, a calcium light attached to it burst into flare and could not be extinguished. This made the float and the officer upon it a brightly illuminated target for an enemy machine-gun some few hundred yards away, which promptly began spitting bullets at full capacity.

Luckily the *Intrepid* was still smoking like a volcano, and thus protected Lieutenant Bonham-Carter somewhat. Seeing a motor-launch pass he caught a rope trailing behind it. The launch towed him through the water until the strain upon his arms became so great he could bear it no longer. At this moment the lieutenant was seen and rescued.

The *Iphigenia*, also fighting, but with only a skeleton crew aboard, followed in the wake of the *Intrepid*, whose smoke blinded her a little. When entering the canal the *Iphigenia* crashed into a dredger with a barge alongside it, that lay moored at the western arm. Through this obstruction she broke a path and went on into the canal pushing the barge before her. Shells and machine-gun bullets were meanwhile whistling all about her from close range. One enemy gunner unconsciously helped the *Iphigenia* considerably. A shell which he fired at the ship cut the pipe of her syren. Through this gash steam came rushing out with a force that drove away the smoke sufficiently for the *Iphigenia* to see what she was doing. According to arrangement her commanding officer, Lieutenant E. W. Billyard-Leake, R.N., backed her on the eastern side of the canal and saw her drop well across channel. Then he blew her up with engines still running to keep the ship in position until she had bedded herself firmly. This accomplished, he and his crew escaped in one of the ubiquitous motor-launches.

Seeing that they were going right into the dragon's mouth, "'An down his throat to choke him,'" as one of the men humorously said, it was regarded as certain that every officer and man in the blocking-ships would be either killed or taken prisoner. But casualties amongst them were very few, and not a single man fell into the enemy's hands. Yet the ships did what they were intended to do.

They completely blocked the mouth of the Bruges Canal "for duration," and there is no likelihood of the enemy clearing it again for a very long time—or at all whilst war lasts. Apart from this serious injury being inflicted upon him by the blocking-ships, the other vessels engaged damaged by gunfire the lock gates which close across the canal entrance, and did much hurt to his shore defences.

CHAPTER 8

The Craft that Kept the Ring

Although they may seem to play a very minor part, the fate of most great combats is largely determined by what may be described as the rank and file of the forces engaged—those who give doughty aid to the champions but are dwarfed almost into invisibility by the resplendent figures of the warrior giants who lead the van. Zeebrugge conformed to the ordinary in this respect. Had it not been for the invaluable services of the monitors, destroyers, motor-launches, and coastal motor-boats which formed the "covering force," the wonderful deeds that gave this expedition its glowing immortality could not have been accomplished.

Particularly courageous was the work done by the motor-launches, which well earned the official acknowledgment given them. These motor-launches are one of the many new types of craft to hoist the white ensign since war began. In truth they little resemble the popular conception of the warship, being nothing more than wooden hulls from 75 to 80 feet in length, fitted with a couple of 220-h.p. internal combustion engines and drawing five foot of water. Each launch carries two Royal Naval Volunteer Reserve officers, two engineers, and five deck-hands.

The M.L.'s, as they are usually termed, may be considered as the R.N.V.R. unit of our fleet. Many of their officers come from the Overseas Dominions, especially Canada and New Zealand. Frail though they be, one finds these motor-launches busy in many seas. In connexion with the Dover Patrol they are largely employed in patrol work and along the Belgian coast making smokescreens for other ships. In that capacity they have participated in nearly every one of the numerous bombardments there.

This and rescue work formed their chief duties at Zeebrugge, where the success of the attack depended upon the smokescreen being properly maintained. The M.L.'s which put up before the enemy's eyes this barrier against visibility were strung out from two miles along the coast to right into the shore, and therefore full in the muzzles of enemy guns, one shell from any one of which hitting a launch would have been enough to blow her out of existence. Some of the launches were only a quarter of a mile from the beach and subjected to the fire of twenty or thirty heavy guns and forty or fifty pom-poms.

Whilst the *Vindictive* was alongside the Mole four of these launches hung around her to protect her against seaward attack. After she drew off they made the smokescreen that enabled the *Vindictive*, the *Iris*, and the *Daffodil* to get away. Also, launches went right into the canal mouth along with the blocking-ships, and that was a plucky thing for such cockle-shell vessels to do, as those aboard them were continually drenched by the splashes from shell which exploded in the water all about them. When the *Thetis* grounded at the canal entrance and became a point-blank target for German guns, M.L. 526, commanded by Lieutenant H. Littleton, R.N.V.R., dashed alongside her, took off her crew as the *Thetis* was sinking and got safely away with them.

Even more thrilling was the ordeal of M.L. 282 (Lieutenant P. T. Deane, R.N.V.R.). She followed the *Intrepid* and *Iphigenia* into the canal itself, and waited under heavy fire until the task of sinking was completed; then she hurried to the ships and took off their crews. Now a motor-launch has only limited passenger accommodation, and by the time "282" completed her rescue journey she had aboard her 109 officers and men from the blocking-ships.

"Overloaded" conveys only a feeble idea of her condition; she was weighted down to the water-line with her heavy freight.

THE UPPER WORKS OF THE *VINDICTIVE*. HERE IS SEEN THE HEAVILY PADDED STRUCTURE ABOVE THE BRIDGE AND ON RIGHT A STEEL FLAME-THROWING STRUCTURE.

Men were clinging to her decks much as a cluster of newly swarmed bees cover anything upon which they alight. Trouble ensued because the launch would not steer properly; she became nearly unmanageable. Instead of making a straight course out of harbour she persisted in turning in towards the Mole and going along close beneath it, where she ran the gauntlet of all the enemy guns left in action, and these were far too numerous to make the over-burdened M.L.'s passage under their muzzles a comfortable one.

Subsequently it was found that the boat would not answer her helm because, owing to the packed state of her decks, many of the "passengers" were standing on the rudder-lines and thus preventing these from moving. Possibly this was a fortunate mishap, as it led to the M.L. going so near the Mole that enemy gunners were confused in their aim and could not at first bring their heavy pieces to bear directly upon her. But in going out of the harbour "282" caught it badly.

Twenty or thirty of the rescued crews aboard her were killed or wounded by the enemy's fire. Her coxswain was killed at the wheel, and Lieutenant K. Wright, R.N.V.R., second in command, severely wounded; yet he stuck courageously at his post, passing back word that he was busily attending to an injured man, when, as a matter of fact, he had himself been so badly hit that for a long time it was thought he could not recover. Eventually "282" reached the *Warwick* (Sir Roger Keyes' flagship) and transferred the rescued to her.

Naturally a flotilla of such light craft as the M.L.'s did not spend a long period amidst the tornado of shell-fire that swept the water at Zeebrugge without suffering casualties, though their losses were infinitesimal in comparison with what might have been expected. The destroyers also got off lightly. One of them, the *North Star*, fell a victim to the enemy's guns. However, a consort, the *Phoebe* (Commander H. E. Gore-Langton, R.N.), slipped in and took off the *North Star's* crew before the destroyer went down.

Whilst engaged doing this a shell struck the *Phoebe's* whistle

THE BLOCK-HOUSE OF THE COMMANDER OF THE *VINDICTIVE*

and started it blowing; nor could it be shut off until sometime after. The noise signalled the position of the destroyer to the enemy, who brought every gun to bear upon her and damaged her considerably. Under the fierce attack the *Phoebe* went calmly on with her rescue work fighting the enemy with one hand, picking up survivors with the other until she had them all aboard. The two destroyers just mentioned and the *Warwick* were detailed to keep sentinel over the *Vindictive*, so that the enemy destroyers which were known to be at sea could not dash through the smoke arid assail her. It was whilst doing this that the *North Star*, blinded by the dense clouds of artificial fog that were rolling about, came suddenly into a patch of water lit up vividly by star-shells and was sunk.

The coastal motor-boats whirled joyously into the very heart of the fray and they were the strangest as well as the swiftest craft that joined in it. These C.M.B.'s are gossamer-like hulls that skim the surface of the water rather than swim upon it; being very lightly powered and of the lightest possible construction, they can spin about with extraordinary speed and nimbleness. All that can be seen of one whilst she is travelling at high power is a pointed bow standing bolt upright amidst a rapidly moving smother of boiling white foam; should there be any sea on, nothing is discernible beyond a high column of flying spray somewhere in the midst of which the boat is buried.

Yet the C.M.B.'s are admirable fighters, capable of doing varied sorts of service. Under such conditions as prevailed at Zeebrugge the enemy found them to be elusive antagonists, swift to strike themselves yet difficult to hit back at, as no sooner had they delivered their blow than they sped away to some other point of attack. The C.M.B.'s raked over the shore close in for whatever they might find there and buzzed about inside the Mole after the fashion of angry hornets.

One of them leaped at the Brussels and torpedoed her; others attacked with Lewis guns the enemy by the seaplane-sheds on the Mole; another spun round the end of the Mole itself and drove a torpedo into a German destroyer that was trying to get at the *Vindictive*. Here, there, and everywhere raced these vicious little craft, worrying an enemy who knows them well and hates them mightily themselves finding greatest safety in their own celerity of movement and the smallness of the target they made.

From the above it will be seen that whilst the chief honours of Zeebrugge fell to the *Vindictive*, to Submarine C3, and to the blocking-ships, each of which did a thing that in itself was sufficient to make the fight for ever illustrious in the annals of sea warfare, the crews manning the various types of supporting vessels played their part with a skill and courage that helped materially towards the brilliant success attained. To employ a rather hackneyed expression, which means a lot all the same, every officer and man there "worthily upheld the traditions of the great service to which he belonged."

The glorious adventure of Zeebrugge showed the whole world that the British seaman of today is made of the same stout stuff as his forefathers.

CHAPTER 9

The First Attack Upon Ostend

Sir Roger Keyes' scheme of organization was comprehensive. Ostend and Zeebrugge being the two gateways into the narrower parts of the North Sea through which the Germans used to make sallies upon our ships, Sir Roger aimed at closing both these up.

Part of the expedition which he led out on April 23 was under orders to make for Zeebrugge; to the other part had been assigned the task of blocking up Ostend harbour. For the latter purpose the obsolete cruisers *Sirius* and *Brilliant*, filled with cement, were taken along. The plans had been for both parts of the joint expedition to reach their goal at the same time, and the "blocking up" operations at each place to be carried out simultaneously. So far as the times of arrival went the programme was kept with exactness; beyond that, local circumstances intervened to prevent a brilliant tactical conception from being developed exactly as projected.

The force dispatched to Ostend was under Commodore Hubert Lyne, C.M.G., who at the time had charge of the Dunkirk section of the Dover Patrol. Surrounded by their escorts, the *Sirius* and *Brilliant* made for their objective, which they reached promptly at the arranged hour midnight. With that success their good luck ended. Fortune proved their enemy thenceforward until the end. In getting to Ostend Commodore Lyne's force overcame many difficulties.

Through darkness, mist, and rain the ships were obliged to

AERIAL PHOTOGRAPH SHOWING THE POSITION OF THE
BLOCK SHIPS AT ZEEBRUGGES

make their way along a hostile coast where navigation, dangerous enough at all times owing to the shallows, etc., was particularly so on a night of low visibility.

Whatever defects he may have, the German is an alert enemy who neglects nothing that can be turned to his own advantage. None quicker than he to recognize where Nature may be made to help the Hun. And he has not omitted to do all that he can to intensify the difficulties of navigation along the Belgian coast. For this no blame may be laid upon him; it is a legitimate act of warfare but it made reaching Ostend perilous work for our assaulting force, which had to steal warily through minefields, as well as face all the other risks scattered along their way.

From all angles Ostend was the smaller operation of the two. The place itself gave less trouble than did Zeebrugge, being nearer to our sea "look-outs" and not so formidable an enemy base. No ship canal served it from inland, and by no possible means could the Germans make it duplicate Zeebrugge, if that were lost to them.

But both these ports "locked, barred, and bolted" against the enemy meant a heavy blow to him, and the smaller operation was a necessary complement to the greater. Yet the partial success of it mattered far less than a similar result at Zeebrugge would have done; and it was partially successful only in so far as the "blowing up" went, owing to factors which no skill or foresight could have eliminated—although the moral effect of the blow at Ostend, coming at the same moment as the smashing one dealt at Zeebrugge, would have fully justified its being struck had none of our ships got near the harbour.

At both places the scheme of operations had much the same basis. The cover of a smokescreen was necessary to carry it through. When Ostend was reached the motor-launches and other craft put up this screen as arranged, and behind it the blocking-ships steamed towards the harbour. But just at the critical moment the wind changed suddenly, blowing the screen away from the ships and uncovering them to the full view of the enemy, who promptly opened at them with all his guns and turned night into day by means of star-shells and searchlights. Even with this handicap against them the blocking-ships might have found their assigned positions had it not been for the fact that the enemy moved the Stroom Bank buoy a mile out of place at the last moment. Not being aware of what he had done, the ships steered by this navigation mark and were thus thrown off their proper course.

Coastal motor-boats, fully as busy here as at Zeebrugge, in addition to helping with smoke-making flares, which lighted up the ends of the piers, enabled the *Sirius* and the *Brilliant* to pass the buoy. But the unexpected shift of the wind which bared the ships of their enshrouding cover showed them to the enemy with startling distinctness. At the moment of revelation they were within point-blank range of his guns; of this he took full advantage, and battered them unmercifully.

The *Sirius* apparently suffered most. Struck many times, she was already in a sinking condition when she grounded on a bank about four hundred yards east of the piers. There the *Brilliant* brought up nearby her, further progress being impossible. Both ships were blown up at this point and their crews taken off by motor-launches.

By marvellous good fortune practically every officer and man escaped from the blocking-ships unhurt; there were only five casualties a miraculous result having regard to the conditions under which the crews were picked up. The rescue work was done by motor-launches, a number of which were employed on this and various other duties under command of Captain Ian Hamilton Benn, M.P. From the time they discovered them until they sank, the Germans directed a fierce, unceasing fire upon the *Sirius* and the *Brilliant*. Full in the face of this M.L. 283 (Lieutenant-Commander H. R. Hoare, R.N.V.R.) and 276 (Lieutenant R. Bourke, R.N.V.R.) went alongside the two ships and took off the 110 officers and men who were upon them.

Previous to this M.L. 532 had gone alongside the *Brilliant*. Caught there by the full blast of the enemy's fire, the M.L. was damaged so severely that she had to be eventually taken in tow by another motor-launch.

Both "532's" engines were broken, and escaping fumes "gassed" the two mechanics attending upon them. The men were found insensible and carried on deck, where artificial respiration was applied until they recovered. Lieutenant Kirkwood, R.N.V.R., who jumped into the engine-room, was "gassed" also. Owing to the launch's starboard engine starting to go astern as soon as she was struck, "532" backed away, from the *Brilliant*, and made, stern foremost, towards the beach, which lay only about two hundred yards distant. All telegraph signals for the engine to be put over proving abortive, Lieutenant Kirkwood jumped below to stop the engine and then discovered the insensible mechanics.

Before he could do anything much this officer had himself to be rescued from the gas-filled engine-room. For about half an hour "532" limped about with her disabled machinery, fairly under the muzzles of the enemy's guns, and those left combatant aboard her had to handle an almost unmanageable boat and bring round their "gassed" comrades as best they could. The simple facts of such an incident as this are the best picture that could be given of it, for whoever is unable to visualize with their aid the position in which boat and crew found themselves would not be helped much by elaborate description.

At last "532" found aid. For somewhere about an hour after this M.L. 276 stood by her, all the while in close proximity to the shore, and finally took the cripple in tow until her mechanics had recovered sufficiently to get their engines working again. By now daylight was approaching, and both launches knew that unless they could get away before dawn crept over the surface of the waters it would be all up with them. In the end "532" was able to crawl safely back to Dunkirk under her own steam.

Coastal motor-boats as well as motor-launches were engaged close in shore and elsewhere within the sphere of operations throughout the fighting. And these fragile vessels seemed to bear charmed lives. There are fully 120 large pieces of artillery having an effective range of twenty miles in the enemy's shore batteries between Zeebrugge and Ostend; how many smaller weapons such as pom-poms he has mounted there only the enemy himself knows. Guns are clustered more thickly around these ports than anywhere else along the coast-line.

Owing to difficulties of visibility the enemy could not easily find our smaller vessels at Ostend, and for the most part fired over them. But this was not due to "wildness " on his part: he sought his targets assiduously enough. As one means of finding them, he sent up innumerable star-shells; then he tried a kind of blue tracer projectile which spread and shot streams of brilliant light, skipping and dipping about the surface of the water in all directions.

Failing of the result he desired in this way, he put up barrages, varying these rapidly. Sometimes they would be a mile and a half from the shore, sometimes half a mile, sometimes only a quarter of a mile. But the vessels he was endeavouring to hit, through quick manoeuvring and good luck, got clear every time not without being subjected to very close shaves, though.

Plunging shell threw cataracts of water over their decks, drenching to the skin the officers and men upon them. In one case an officer was covered with mud which a projectile, diving in a shallow place, heaved up from the bottom of the harbour. So long as their presence was needed, then, the flotillas stuck to their posts in the shell-pitted water off Ostend; then steamed away, leaving the enemy guns in full action behind them. The task set the force had not been completed; it was merely postponed, not abandoned.

Chapter 10

"Finishing the Job"

It is not the habit of the British Navy to leave a job half finished. Circumstances already explained having prevented the "blocking up" of Ostend on St. George's Day, the Dover Patrol forthwith busied itself with preparations for renewing the attempt at the first favourable opportunity. Nor was the doing of this delayed very long. A new expedition was formed, and on the night of May 9 the *Vindictive*, having won immortality at Zeebrugge some seventeen days earlier, found an honourable grave beneath the waters of Ostend harbour.

The second, and successful, attack upon this place was carried through by a force under Commodore Hubert Lynes, at whose disposal Vice-Admiral Sir Roger Keyes placed all the monitors, destroyers, and other craft he required. As in the two previous ventures of a like nature, all the officers and men taking part were volunteers. Once again the difficulty lay not in getting numbers so much as in selecting from those who offered. Here is an incident that shows the fine spirit of our men.

After the *Vindictive* had steamed to Dunkirk it became necessary to reduce her stokehold complement to the barest minimum so as to lessen casualties, for there was not much hope that any who went into Ostend aboard would come out again alive. But when a weeding-out was attempted none of the crew were willing to leave the ship. At last the matter had to be settled by drawing lots. In this way was decided which stokers should have the coveted, though perilous, honour of remaining in her and

AERIAL PHOTOGRAPH AFTER THE RAID

which should go ashore.

Commander A. E. Godsall, who had had charge of the *Brilliant* in the earlier attempt, was given command of the *Vindictive* upon this occasion. Under him was a volunteer crew drawn from those who had served aboard the Ostend blocking-ships on the previous occasion, save only that Engineer-Lieutenant-Commander W. R. Bury and four engine-room artificers—H, Cavanagh, N. Carrol, A. Thomas, and H. Harris—who had been in the *Vindictive* at Zeebrugge, were at their own request allowed to remain in the ship because of their special knowledge of her engines. Commodore Lynes directed operations from the Faulknor, having with him as aides Commander J. L. C. Clarke, D.S.O., R.N., and Commander H. L. Sandford, D.S.O., R.N.

For some days prior to the operations bad weather had prevented more than the scantiest reconnaissance being done. But the enemy apparently feared that another attempt would be made upon Ostend, for he had removed all buoys so as to impede navigation as much as possible. In arranging the new expedition all possible care was taken to achieve a surprise attack and prevent any hitch from occurring. Aircraft as well as sea-craft were employed, and at one time it looked as though the expedition might have to fight its way through, as whilst it was on its way a force of nine enemy destroyers were reported to be out, though nothing was subsequently seen of these.

A squadron of monitors strung themselves to seaward, and a destroyer screen was also thrown out. Preceded by the coastal motor-boats and motor-launches, each of which had its appointed post, the *Vindictive* made for Ostend, being due there at 2 a.m. She arrived in good time. At 1.43 a.m. the anxiously awaited signal was given. Aeroplanes hovering over Ostend itself repeated the order to the monitors at sea and to the heavy Royal Marine Artillery batteries along the coast. By the next second huge shells were bursting on enemy positions. They screamed in from seaward, they screeched up from the coast, and a hail of bombs from the sky supplemented them. The enemy was given a particularly warm time of it. Forward now shot two G.M.B.'s,

GLORIOUS END OF H.M.S. *VINDICTIVE*

SUSSESSFULLY SUNK AT OSTENDE HARBOUR – MAY 9TH, 1918

commanded by Lieutenant D. Reid, R.N.R., and Lieutenant A. L. Poland, R.N. Straight they went, one at each pier-head, and swished torpedoes into them. Amidst the roar of the explosions which followed upon the weapons striking, an enemy machine-gun situated on the western pier was seen to fly upward as the end of the structure disappeared.

Lieutenant W. R. Slayter, R.N., who was waiting there for the purpose, dropped a calcium flare on the spot where the Stroom buoy should have been anchored, and thus provided the *Vindictive* with a navigating mark which the enemy could not obliterate. Meanwhile the motor-launches had formed up on either hand and made two walls of dense smoke, between which the *Vindictive* passed towards her goal hidden from the eyes of the German artillerymen. But though the latter could not see, they could act—and they did act precipitously. With a deafening crash all their guns leaped quickly into life.

Searchlights peered inquisitively about, trying to pierce the fog-wall that the motor-launches had built; star-shells innumerable made their curious green effects on the thickened atmosphere, whilst "flaming onions" (strings of luminous balls) floated overhead in all directions. The noise was terrific. Amid the hell of shrieking projectiles, the flash of nearby guns, and the unearthly "fireworks" that the enemy was sending up it seemed that surely no vessel could live. Yet the smokescreens served their purpose so admirably that the Germans fired right over our ships, being unable to range them with accuracy.

Now came a change which at first hampered both sides equally. The weather clerk took a hand in the game. At 1.45 a.m. the sky became overcast. Five minutes later there drifted over a real sea fog which made the imitation one look like well, an imitation. So dense was this fog that our destroyers, in order to keep in touch with each other, had to incur the risk of switching on their lights and blowing their syrens. The *Vindictive* found herself absolutely benighted.

All around her lay a pall of blackness which made seeking the harbour mouth a sort of "blind man's buff" game on her part.

She reduced speed and nosed around, first westward, then eastward, unwittingly passing the entrance twice whilst doing this. Then a coastal motor-boat put down on the water a million-candle-power Dover flare. Through the rift which this cut in the fog the *Vindictive* saw the opening between the piers and steamed boldly into the harbour, passing right over the flare that had proved as a lamp to her feet.

Another coastal motorboat hung a flare in the rigging of the sunken *Sirius* to guide the *Vindictive* towards her goal. Under clearer weather conditions this display of dazzling lights would have brought heavy casualties upon our smaller craft inshore by disclosing their whereabouts to the enemy; but the fog, though hampering our ships much, did this good service for them—that it kept the C.M.B.'s and M.L.'s so well enshrouded that the enemy could not discern them by the lights which made brilliant the pathway of the *Vindictive*. Throughout this period of fog and bewilderment the heavy gun attack from monitors and coast batteries proceeded unchecked, as likewise did the overhead bombing. Hard indeed would it be to convey any adequate idea of what the water-front of Ostend resembled whilst the affair was at its greatest intensity. A thousand fiends playing wild gambols in the air could scarcely have raised such an appalling clatter.

No sooner had the *Vindictive* got inside the piers than the enemy guns began punishing her ruthlessly. Fired from short range, the shells ripped open old wounds in her structure and inflicted many new ones. Over her decks and upper works swept a deadly torrent of steel. A shell struck the after-control, instantly killing Sub-Lieutenant A. H. MacLachlan and all others in the place. Bullets from machine-guns came in such showers that they made the chart-room untenable.

Consequently Commander Godsall and his officers went into the armoured conning-tower, from whence they steered the ship. There was a gap in the eastern pier about two hundred yards from its seaward end, caused possibly by a collision, or it may have been one of several breaches in the piers made by the enemy to prevent us from landing upon them an attacking party as we did at Zeebrugge. Just after passing the spot Commander Godsall went outside the conning-tower and stationed himself just in front of it so that he could better see the *Vindictive's* course. Through the observation-slit in the tower he gave the order to "Starboard helm." This was obeyed: as a result of it the *Vindictive* placed her nose towards the eastern pier and began to swing across the channel she was designed to block.

Just at that moment a shell from the shore batteries struck full on the conning-tower, killing Commander Godsall and stunning Lieutenant Sir John Alleyne, the navigating officer who was by the wheel inside. Through the observation-slit Lieutenant V. A. C. Crutchley, R.N., the only uninjured officer in the tower, called to the commander.

Receiving no reply from him, Lieutenant Crutchley put the engine hard astern to assist in swinging the *Vindictive* athwart channel. By this time she was pointing at an angle of about forty degrees from the pier, grounded so fast that she could not be moved farther. For some few minutes Lieutenant Crutchley tried to do so but failed; thereupon he gave the order to clear the engine-rooms and abandon ship.

Engineer-Lieutenant-Commander Bury, the last one below, blew the main charges from aft whilst Lieutenant Crutchley blew the auxiliary ones from his station in the conning-tower. By the force of the explosion the bottom plates were ripped out of the ship, her bulk-head torn down, and with one frail quiver the *Vindictive* sank six feet until she lay fast on the bottom of the Channel. Lieutenant Crutchley searched the ship in the hopes of finding the bodies of Commander Godsall and Sub-Lieutenant MacLachlan, but her decks were such a tangle of wreckage that he could discover no trace of either.

M.L. 254 (Lieutenant G. H. Drummond, R.N.V.R.) now went alongside the *Vindictive*, which the enemy were still bombarding furiously, and took off her crew—a dangerous task, during the performance of which the M.L. suffered considerably. But exemplary bravery and coolness were shown by everybody.

First-class Petty Officer J. J. Reed, the *Vindictive's* coxswain, scrambled through the heavy fire into the conning-tower, and brought from thence Lieutenant Sir John Alleyne, who was still unconscious. Before he could be lifted into the launch Sir John Alleyne was hit and fell into the water. As Engineer-Lieutenant Bury was leaving the *Vindictive* he too sustained bad wounds. He rolled over and over along the rescuing boat's deck with enemy machine-gun bullets continually striking him. In all "254" saved two officers and thirty-eight men—a magnificent feat considering her own battered condition.

As she followed the *Vindictive* into harbour a shell struck her, killing the second in command, Lieutenant Gordon Ross, R.N.V.R., who was spraying the pier-ends with bullets from a machine-gun, and a deck hand named Thomas. Lieutenant Drummond was wounded severely in the right leg, and Rees, the coxswain, had part of his hand shot away as he stood at the wheel.

A second later and Lieutenant Drummond got a machine-gun bullet in his shoulder and another through his right arm, whilst a third injured his hand badly. Nevertheless he and the coxswain both stuck to their posts, taking the M.L. alongside the *Vindictive* and away again after she had picked up the crew. Stern foremost, they backed the launch out of the harbour and got to sea.

It was there found that the vessel had suffered so much damage that difficulty was experienced in keeping her afloat; practically she was in a sinking condition. But they managed, by means of pumping, to make her float for half an hour longer, at the end of which time they fell in with the destroyer *Warwick*, with Vice-Admiral Sir Roger Keyes aboard. To the *Warwick* were transferred all those in the launch and the launch herself was sunk, it being clear that she could not in any circumstances hold the surface much longer.

M.L. 276 (Lieutenant R. Bourne, R.N.R.) had also followed the *Vindictive* in. As "254" left her "276" went alongside her to make sure nobody had been left aboard; getting no reply to his shouts, Lieutenant Bourne began to back away. Thinking he heard a cry, he took his vessel to the *Vindictive* again, but once more could find nobody. A second and a third time this happened, Lieutenant Bourne being all the while under intensive enemy machine-gun fire. Already his launch had been hit by a shell and the coxswain killed at the wheel, his place there being taken by Sub-Lieutenant Petrie.

Going for the third time alongside the *Vindictive*, Lieutenant Bourne found in the water beside her, clinging to a rope, three men; it was their cries for help that he had answered so often. When Sub-Lieutenant Petrie had hauled them aboard it was found that one of the rescued trio was Lieutenant Sir James Alleyne, whom falling into the water had brought sufficiently to consciousness for him to grasp a rope. M.L. 276 literally fought her way out of harbour, as Sub-Lieutenant Petrie kept a machine-gun spitting at the piers whilst she ran past them.

What a hot corner "276" had been in was evinced by the condition of her hull. There were over fifty shots in this, part of her wheel was blown away, and a five-inch shell had gone clean through her—fortunately without exploding. Two other launches that entered the harbour for rescue work also experienced a bad time there, but got away in the end.

As regards the object of the expedition, this was attained in so far as the *Vindictive* was concerned. She lies in a position which blocks the channel so that no large craft can get by. Ostend as a naval base is now of much less value to the Hun.

Chapter 11

The Hot Triangle

The Hot Triangle lies about fifteen minutes' air voyage of England. Do not confound it with the Wet Triangle; they are quite distinct war zones. One of several differences between them is that, whilst warships dominate in the Wet Triangle, most of the fighting in the Hot Triangle is done by aircraft. Roughly, a line cutting through the sea just off Nieuport-Ostend-Zeebrugge marks the base of the "Triangle"; its apex lies at Bruges.

Not exactly a triangular dimension! Maybe so; but why urge such a quibble? It's one near enough to justify the name. Besides, this is no book of *Euclid* but a volume concerned rather with what happens in an area than with the label colloquially attached to it.

And what happens in the bomb-wracked terrain of the Hot Triangle affects home folk very closely. The farthermost (in some ways the most effective) outposts of London's protection against aerial attacks lie there; also, to an important extent, there begins the defence of our sea-borne commerce, and of the Ports of America too, against U-boat depredations.

It is a commonplace of strategy that the best way of preventing your enemy from striking you at close quarters is to keep him busy shielding his own body. By acting on this principle our forces operating against the Hun in the Hot Triangle save people living this side of the North Sea from many unpleasant visitations.

Owing to geographical conditions the aircraft attached to

the Dover Patrol find greater opportunities here than its ships do. The latter keeps a strangle-hold to seaward. But warships are unable to go overland; aircraft can do that. Shoal-water and shore-lines do not restrict their radius of action; trenches cannot be dug against them; neither can barbed-wire entanglements stay their progress, nor minefields hamper their movements.

Added to this, the "overhead arm" is the most mobile of all—usually the most far-reaching as well. Daily it stretches into various parts of the Hot Triangle and delivers lusty blows at the enemy, who in quaking terror signals around, "Take cover, take cover. Here are those *Verdammte Englischer* aeroplanes coming again. *Gott strafe 'em*"—and down goes the Hun rabbit into his burrow.

Do not look on this as a fancy picture, for it is not one. If there be anything certain in this world it is the fact that the persistent bombing raids made by our aerial squadrons in this part of Flanders have "put the wind up the enemy" pretty badly. Their attacks upon him are unceasing. Every possible day finds them on wing.

Every possible night also—plans being so arranged that raids are continuous; they begin with daybreak and they don't stop with darkness. Certain squadrons "go over" at different times during the day loaded with bombs and deliver their cargo upon a chosen objective; others attack only at night. Never does the enemy know when they are coming nor where they will hit him.

The only certain thing he knows is that they will assuredly come sometime, and this purposely created suspense tries his nerves severely. One time the target will be Bruges, another Ostend, another Zeebrugge, or some point of military importance lying in the immediate vicinity of these places.

Great care is always taken to assault only actual military objectives. The residential parts of a Flanders town are never bombed by our airmen.

Neither do they copy the Germans' practice of throwing projectiles about indiscriminately. Upon munition centres, wharves, aerodromes, and other legitimate points they shower deadly missiles actually by ton-weights at a time and content themselves with this.

Photographs show Bruges docks to have been bombed by us so heavily that the space around them resembles a piece of honeycomb laid flat, so full of holes is it. Yet the town itself remains untouched. The same is true of Ostend and elsewhere.

If the Powers who have the ordering of affairs were willing that they should do so—and they are not—the men who handle our aerial fleets would decline to lower themselves to the contemptible level of the Hun.

Except for the coming and going of the machines their daylight incursions into the Hot Triangle yield little to the mere sightseer. But night-bombing raids furnish a wonderfully picturesque spectacle. Sitting amongst sand-dunes or at the edge of the flooded area, one sees approaching what seem like huge, staring owls' eyes high up in the air.

These are the navigation lights of the big bombing craft. After a while the angry whirr of the machines sounds overhead. Gradually this noise fades into the distance and the pyrotechnic display begins. The enemy has heard his sorely dreaded enemies coming and forthwith provides for them the warmest reception he can.

He goes to the business whole-heartedly, and does it with real Teuton thoroughness. On every hand shrapnel-bursts dot the sky with brilliant star-points of light; often there's quite a Milky Way of them. Flares go up one after the other in rapid succession; then "onions" by the string; then tracer-bullets thread long lines in the darkness. Across this flat country, which offers no obstacles to the vision, one can obtain as good a view of the "fireworks" over such places as Ostend and Bruges as if one were close by them. Also of the searchlights, which appear to be uncountable; these shoot up suddenly like thick forests of tall, silvery, branchless trees.

And the noise grows terrific. "Whing," "whing," sings the shrapnel from the "Archies." Down come the bombs with a thunderous "Wonk, wonk," shaking the ground as they explode. Fires start up—this is a quite usual result—and to the "hate" with which the Hun tortures the air overhead is added the blaze and rolling fumes of the conflagrations beneath.

Quite often an ammunition-dump, or something else equally combustible, is fired, and the roar of its explosion momentarily drowns all other noises. Scenes of this kind are of almost nightly occurrence within the Hot Triangle. If Bruges escapes, Zeebrugge gets it; whilst Ostend is rarely exempt, being a convenient target for our airmen to take a parting shot at.

What these unceasing raids have cost the enemy in the loss of war material he alone knows; but the sum must be tremendous. For enormous damage has been done to him. In addition to destroying his ammunition-dumps and wrecking his aerodromes we, by thus attacking him from the air, make it impossible for him to use against us the huge stores of war material he is constantly accumulating in the "Triangle."

What is equally important, we prevent him from doing anything towards unsealing Zeebrugge or from obtaining much military benefit from his possession of the Flanders canal system. All the waterways within the Hot Triangle are regularly searched by our aircraft. Wherever they find a destroyer pushed away for safety they bomb it. Submarines, munition barges, and so on get like treatment. Nowhere can the enemy find a safe corner to stow anything. Even half-subterranean aerodromes are spied out and "pilled."

Big gun positions, naturally, are much too tempting objectives to be let alone. The Hun artillerymen employed about them are being continually chased into their dugouts like rabbits chevied to their holes. Much of their time is spent in building new shelters to replace those we make untenable.

Until the Royal Air Force came into being the Royal Naval Air Service did most of the air work in this sector. Ex-R.N.A.S. flights are still the most numerous there. It may be only a fortuitous circumstance or the same thing may be true of other divisions of the R.A.F., but into the personnel of these squadrons there has been introduced a composite material that results in splendid efficiency.

Pilots and observers are drawn in nearly equal proportions from the Motherland and the Overseas Dominions, particularly Canada; in some cases a few American flying men are attached as well. Just as the finest metals are obtained by blending various ores, so this combination of men, differing in some ways but fundamentally of the same blood and the same ideals, has produced a magnificent body of airmen.

Moreover, they work excellently together. It is the squadron rather than the individual which they think about. With them the job counts more than the man who does it. Assimilation has reached such a point amongst them that they have even arrived at a common language in which Colonial and American idioms figure largely. For example, no airman hereabout ever says "Yes"; "Yep" is the affirmative he always uses.

Many other indications are observable of the complete and harmonious understanding that has been established. Comradeship in danger is the greatest bond for knitting men together; and the Allies' pilots have it in full strength here.

Well need they be competent. In the Hot Triangle the enemy has mustered as formidable a collection of "Archies" and other anti-aircraft weapons as can be found anywhere along the Western Front; the whole area is stiff with them. Yet despite this, our airmen and their American comrades cross the lines at will. Quite commonly they go forty or more miles into hostile territory—forcing the fighting always, never declining combat however long the odds may be against them numerically.

Often these odds are two to one, as the Hun never chances a "scrap" in the air when numbers are anything like equal. Nor will he come near the lines for an engagement. His favourite practice is to wait in force anywhere from twenty to forty miles behind them and try to cut off stragglers from our formations, bearing them down by sheer weight of numbers. When our bombers go out upon daylight expeditions they are accompanied by fighting squadrons composed of lighter machines. The task assigned to the latter is to hold off the enemy aircraft whilst the bombers do their work.

Only occasionally does the enemy attack. He sits up in the air as high as he can get and watches for an opportunity of swooping down when conditions are all in his favour. If he cannot get these advantages he will avoid a fight when—he has the chance of doing so; that is not always afforded him.

As soon as their cargo has been delivered our bombers and scouts together invariably make for any machines that may be within striking distance and bring them to action if by any possibility they can do this.

Night raids are a different matter. Then the machines steal in and steal out again without escort; for various reasons such would be of little value after the sun has gone to bed. Being brave enough in the dark, the Hun airmen take advantage of the cover of night to come our side of the lines and try reprisals.

Generally he aims at "laying out" one of the aerodromes from which we send the machines that trouble him so sorely; but he never succeeds in diminishing the force of our aerial offensive, though he spends quite a lot of money trying to accomplish that object. During one of these nocturnal assaults he has, upon occasion, expended somewhere about one hundred thousand pounds' worth of bombs without damaging a single one of our machines or hurting any of the men who fly them.

And he is not permitted to raid with impunity. The whirr of the Gotha overhead is a signal that breaks pandemonium loose. Guns roar out, not by twos and threes, but by batteries; not over a few miles, but many. "Mournful Marie" wails her dismal note of warning to Dunkirk. Syrens, shrill and piercing, repeat the "alert" elsewhere, whilst "Archies" emphasize it by their ear-splitting "cracks." Within the Hot Triangle war blazes fiercely in the sky and beats a destructive tattoo on the ground.

Just our side of the lines there prevails a similar "liveliness" in so far as the air is concerned. Nor is this merely an incidental state of affairs; it is the normal condition every night when the weather permits flying. Out of sheer desperation the Hun seizes every chance of "getting a bit of his own back"; but in this locality, at any rate, what he succeeds in doing to us is only a mere trifle in comparison with what our airmen do to him.

By their skill and persistency they have made the Triangle a hard place for the Hun to live in, though for strategic reasons he dare not evacuate it. So he hangs on tremblingly each day fearing what the night will bring, each night hoping that clouds and mist will next day give him a temporary respite from the assaults of our bombing squadrons.

CHAPTER 12

The Airmen's Part in Ostend Fight

For the student of war Ostend possesses one feature of out-standing interest. It supplied the first instance of sea-fleets and air-fleets being employed jointly, under the same commander, in such an assault upon an enemy stronghold. Events at which we have barely leisure to glance in these crowded days are certain at some future time to be weighed in the balances of history and their importance correctly appraised.

Probably the real significance of the innovation made at Os-tend may have to await this judgment before receiving full rec-ognition, but the most casual follower of "the greatest game of all" cannot wholly overlook its import. Earth, sea, and sky were marshalled against Hun, for land guns as well as others played their part on our side.

Such a co-ordination of forces was made possible by the fact that the Dover Patrol is not limited wholly to the sea. Within its sphere comes a part of the English coast, a part of the Bel-gian coast, and a part of the French coast, as well as the water that lies between them. Both sea-squadrons and air-squadrons are included in the Patrol's effectives. All are under command of Vice-Admiral Sir Roger Keyes, who thus had at his disposal the means of attacking the enemy from sea and air at the same moment. As both "wings" were directed by one clear- thinking mind, risk of confusion disappeared; that was a great advantage. Ostend, in this respect, proved the value of unity of control.

Usually the best recorder of an event is a person who has

taken part in it—someone who, possessing the gift of narrative, sets down his impressions of things seen whilst yet they are fresh in his mind.

The following account of what our aircraft did at Ostend on May 9, and what befell them whilst doing it, was contributed by a pilot who took part in the fight. His story is given with only this prefatory comment:

Any person whose imagination cannot be quickened into some comprehension of what it must have been like to sit up in the air and watch the night-battle raging below must be exceedingly sluggish-minded. Could one conceive a more enthralling situation than that of our airmen, who from their cloud-paved eyrie looked down upon this picture of hot-breathed war—upon a combat in which they themselves were to the enemy the most terrifying element because they represented the peril that flew unseen?

By employing aircraft to escort the fleet and thus prevent enemy scouts from detecting its movements," says the narrator, "we were enabled to spring a real surprise attack upon the Hun. I was with the bombing squadrons. When we turned out to make a start the weather did not seem very propitious. After 'running up' our engines to warm them and see that they were all right, we climbed into our seats. Then came the order to 'go,' and off we went. Clouds were low and there were confusing mists, but we knew the way so well from having gone over it often that we could have steered straight for Ostend blindfold. Climbing gradually higher and higher, we sped through the night at a high pace. It was so dark that in order to avoid colliding with each other our navigation lights had to be kept burning; that was a handicap, though not a very material one since it merely set the Hun guessing. He might be able to see us coming but did not know whither we were bound.

Each of us knew exactly where to go and what to do;

fully detailed instructions were in our hands. As a result, we made our rendezvous easily in spite of the weather difficulties. One of our chief objectives was to occupy the enemy's attention—to keep him so busy looking after us that he would have no leisure to spare for investigations seaward. We did that successfully. Furthermore, the distraction we caused prevented him from using many of his guns and searchlights on the fleet. Clever as he is, the Hun has not yet produced a gun that will fire two ways at once; nor a searchlight that can look two ways at once either. Everything turned on us meant something diverted from the ships. It was largely as a result of this distraction that the fleet was able to approach undetected. After arriving at our destination we flew round and round, waiting the signal to begin operations. Now 'marking time' in the air on a dark night over a strongly defended enemy base is a manoeuvre one must perform before one can understand what it's like. As I have already mentioned, weather conditions were against us. Although our navigation lights were on we had several narrow escapes from collisions. Often we got quite close to the ships; then buzzed off again before they spotted us.

So things went on until we received the anxiously awaited signal; this came from the monitors lying far out at sea. As soon as we saw their guns begin to make big rents of vivid yellow light in the darkness that lay like a funeral pall over the water we knew the moment had arrived for us to start attacking. These gun-flashes were our word of command, and gladly we obeyed it. In fact, the boom of the monitors' guns proved a call to general activity. The sleeping blackness beneath us woke suddenly into virile, noisy life. Our own coastal batteries began popping in shells from long range; whilst the Hun commenced to use everything he had—and that was quite a lot—with spiteful energy. And we knew, though we could not see them, that somewhere near at hand a whole swarm of our ships were creeping silently up to join the melee. One felt a certain sense of pleasurable expectancy whilst waiting for them to burst in.

We climbed and turned our machines towards the shore. Immediately the guns from our monitors and batteries opened up the Hun started his customary fireworks. From the altitude we were at we could see not much of Ostend itself except the enemy's 'Archie' bursts and 'flaming onions,' which were soon flying about everywhere. These 'onions' are rather ghastly sort of things. I don't know whether they are intended merely for illuminating or for setting machines on fire as well. They do the illuminating right enough. As a string of these luminous green balls goes wriggling by it makes one feel so lit up that every button on one's coat must be visible to the anti-aircraft gunners decidedly an uncomfortable sensation. Besides, a pilot would be severely burned, if nothing worse, should an 'onion' hit his bus. Searchlights were switched on also. In short, one way or another there was as fine a display of 'pyrotechny' as one could wish to see.

Right into the middle of this we sailed. It was our job to go there—and we went, without thinking overmuch about what might result from the venture. So quickly did matters develop that by the time we passed across the beach the air was fairly vibrating with 'hate' of one kind or another. 'Old man Hun,' as my Canadian observer calls him, was throwing it up with both hands and all too bountifully.

Unquestionably he was in a panic, and, as he always does when in that state of mind, he started a barrage that seemed powerful enough to lift the ceiling. So great was the noise that we could hear very little even with engines merely 'ticking'; but from long acquaintance with the sound we recognized the unpleasant whistle of shrapnel as it sprayed out around us. This ugly 'dust' seemed to be blowing about in clouds on every hand. Several of our buses were hit,

SOME OF THE CREW OF THE *VINDICTIVE* AMONG THE DEBRIS.

though, luckily, the men in them got through unhurt. Our situation was pretty tough. 'Archies' and 'onions' were not the only troubles we had to contend against. Searchlights no one minded much; the clouds screened us from them. One of our greatest difficulties was the disturbed air. Piloting a bus through it resembled navigating a choppy, storm-tossed sea. This atmospheric condition resulted from the firing beneath us. Big shells were constantly whizzing in from our monitors in one direction and from our coastal batteries in another, to say nothing of those coming from enemy artillery. Every time a projectile passed beneath us it caused our machines to bump and wallow exactly as a ship does in the trough of a heavy sea. As projectiles by the score were criss-crossing unceasingly, you may imagine what a rough passage we made overhead. We were like a squadron of ships fighting in a gale. That may appear a strange comparison, though it's as accurate a one as could be made. One could hardly have had conditions worse for piloting.

We were not mere spectators of the fray; we took a combatant part in it as well. In addition to acting as a sort of decoy for turning the enemy's attention one way, the air squadrons were detailed for lighting up and bombing enemy gun-positions. To do this we circled over his defences and dropped parachute-flares upon them. These flares illuminate a considerable area; they are very brilliant and burn for a long time. As they go sailing slowly earthward everything in the vicinity of them shows up clearly almost startlingly so, owing to the queer sheen of the light.

We used this device for disclosing enemy gun-positions to our ships. Steering our buses over the Hun's gun-emplacements, we dropped parachute-flares just rearward of them. As the flares descended so they threw the gun-positions into strong relief. You know how an object shows up in the darkness when a light is placed behind it; that is how the Hun batteries looked, and they thus made a vividly outstanding target for our artillery. After releasing the flares we dropped bombs. Our course took us over and over the enemy defences, where we dropped flares one minute and bombs the next. For about an hour this went on almost incessantly, whilst the Hun did his best—no mean best either—to bring our machines down.

Sitting up amongst the clouds and watching the fight below, in brief intervals between taking part in it ourselves, was a weird kind of experience. None could see us, though we could see, more or less, what was going on all round. It was by no means an easy seat that we had, either. All the while the enemy 'Archied'' us hotly; 'onions' flamed up, and the big guns slung about their ton-weight shells, which as they passed underneath caused our buses to bump and roll frightfully. Visibility was fluky; once we could barely see objects one hundred feet away. One had an odd kind of impression that the fighting we surveyed was taking place under a great black veil that had a big rent in it just where we hung; through that rent hell blazed up fiercely and viciously. Except for this spot, on looking round one felt a queer sense of the unreal. You must remember that the flashes of the guns out at sea, along the coast, and in the harbour were at times only faintly visible to us through the murk; then they would become quite vivid again.

Occasionally, as we shut off engines to steal down towards an objective the full roar of battle came upon our ears; and it was an awful din too. Guns barking, projectiles exploding, shells shrieking, shrapnel whining past us—how can one describe the indescribable?

For about an hour, as I have already said, we were amidst these surroundings—full in the midst of them, with no chance of getting away and no wish to do so. We dropped flares, bombed gun-positions, hovered about over beach and harbour; circled out of the fray, then flew into it again, carrying out our orders.

None of our machines failed to see the business through to the end. I am sure that no man in them would willingly have done otherwise. The main question in our minds was how to worry the Hun hard enough to keep his attention off our ships, or reduce to a minimum all of it he could spare for them. Busy as they were in other ways, some of the fellows thought out special methods of doing this. Switching off engines, they dived noiselessly towards his batteries, gave them a burst of machine-gun fire, then 'zoomed' up out of reach before the enemy could get a shot at them; others slid down the beams of searchlights and fired at the lenses.

Each one of us aimed at planting our bombs where they would do most good from our point of view, and we went low enough to ensure a fair shot before we released them. It was exciting work, and more than a bit dangerous. But one does not trouble over the dangers incurred when in the heat of battle. Think of the sporting side of the thing. That is the way to get through with a good heart and a whole skin. Anyway, that was the aspect of the matter that appealed most to us.

Regarded in that light it was a great event. Your own wit and skill pitted against the enemy's; as a result, either he gets you or you get him. That is the stake you play for always, and it's big enough to give wonderful zest to the game. Your life or your liberty: can you imagine a stake that is bigger or so much worth endeavouring to win! It was not from any lack of hard trying that the Hun failed to 'get' any of us; always his powerful searchlights were trying to pick us up.

But a searchlight can only look one way at a time, and whilst peering about after us they could not be turned seaward. Another point of the game scored in our favour. The weather aided us by limiting the searchlight's range. It was queer to look down from above the clouds and see them turned into a luminous yellow mass right below you by the lights that made persistent yet unsuccessful attempts to pierce through them queer—but encouraging, being a distinct advantage to us. For no airman likes to have the rays of the Ostend searchlight encompass him; such an occurrence is a sure prelude of a hot burst of 'Archies' close under your wings.

Knowing the main objective of the operations, I kept an eye upon the harbour entrance, as I believe all of us did, to see the *Vindictive* come in. Somehow we never doubted her getting there. Owing to the fog, mist, and darkness we could not obtain a clear view of what the ships were doing, though we knew from the heavy firing that they had arrived and were hotly engaged. Suddenly a big flare illuminated the space between the piers and the *Vindictive* showed at the entrance, making inward. Immediately she appeared the fierce heart of the fighting, if I may so express myself, seemed to switch sharply from the coast-line to the harbour.

How many guns the enemy brought into action here I do not know; they blazed from shore and piers with one incessant roar. He seemed to sweep every inch of the harbour with them. Gazing down upon it, the combat seemed to me so incredibly furious that none could survive it. You can have no conception of what a cyclone of destruction appeared to have burst upon that small space; neither can those who were caught in it, for the comprehensive, detached view we obtained from aloft was impossible to them.

So long as the affair lasted I looked and marvelled. It was an intensely fascinating spectacle—the more so as one knew it to be war. real blood-stirring, blood-spilling, death-dealing war, that one was looking at, not merely some cleverly staged make-believe.

We see quite a bit of war in this corner of the front, but I had never laid eyes upon anything in the fighting way nearly so thrilling as this; possibly I may never do so again, for you cannot have 'Ostends' very often—even with the whole world at enmity. Of the details of the fighting we could distinguish nothing; only the picture as a whole spread under our eyes. The impression of it which I brought away was of booming guns; blazing searchlights with tiny dots of vessels shooting through their rays; all sorts of weird illuminations floating about overhead; clouds of smoke with great swathes of fire cutting through them; bursting shells; noise incredible.

Surrounding this picture of flaming, hot, intensive war, night lay like a broad ebony frame. 'The burial of the *Vindictive*' one of our fellows termed it; and that would certainly make an appropriate title to the picture, remembering what the gallant old ship had done. When the tumult quietened down and the fleet drew off, leaving the *Vindictive* in her honourable grave, we turned homeward also.

Except for some of the machines being shot up a little, our squadrons suffered no damage. Pretty lucky that, considering the fierce onslaught they had withstood from enemy 'Archies.' But with our return to camp aircraft had by no means finished with Ostend. A few hours after we left other of our squadrons were over the place worrying the Hun—and they have kept this sport going ever since.

CHAPTER 13

Some Stories of Our War Eagles

Rome's war eagles were carried on the tops of poles. Great Britain's war eagles fly—and there are quite a lot of them always on the wing over the Hot Triangle.

As might be expected, in their raids into such a stoutly defended area our airmen meet with many thrilling adventures. One cannot help being impressed with their calm acceptance as being just "part of a day's work" of situations that would freeze an ordinary person's blood into icicles by the sheer horror of them. For cool nerve here is an incident that would be difficult to beat.

During a night raid one of our big bombers had beaten up "good and proper," as the phrase goes, a troublesome enemy aerodrome within the Triangle to the accompaniment of the customary virulent defensive gun-play from the ground. Driven by this to a high altitude, the machine continued circling round seeking a place upon which its remaining "eggs" could be laid to advantage, when the gunner in the back seat espied a hostile aeroplane beneath him. Determined that this should not go unassailed, he unshipped his Lewis gun and, leaning over the side, fired straight down at the foe.

When all his cartridges were spent the gunner straightened himself up to reload. At that instant he noticed a leak in one of the petrol-pipes. A piece of shrapnel from an anti-aircraft gun had struck the pipe and cut a big hole in it. The gunner could not speak to the pilot from his cockpit, so he dropped the Lewis into this, climbed out on top of the fuselage and wriggled his way along the top of it. The bomber being now some ten or twelve thousand feet up, the gunner had to make his way at this dizzy height for some distance along a slippery domed surface, crawling right beneath the upper planes and between the propellers.

A bank of the machine or the slightest slip on his part would have projected him into space. Unmindful of his own danger, the gunner crept forward until he was able to lean over the pilot's seat and shout into his ear "Your petrol-tank is leaking." The pilot signalled acknowledgment of this information, which was soon after further impressed upon him by one engine ceasing to run through lack of fuel. He switched it off and struggled home with only one engine working.

Nor was this the sum total of troubles. A change in the weather caused the aneroid to register wrongly; the instrument showed an altitude of some hundreds of feet where actually there were only tens. As a result of this, whilst the pilot was making, as he thought, for the beach, the machine struck the water with great force and turned over. In his hurry to climb along and tell the pilot about the leaking pipe the gunner had forgotten to secure the Lewis. Consequently, as the machine somersaulted the gun rolled forward, striking on the head, first the pilot, then the observer who sat beside him.

Both received nasty injuries. Seeing what had happened, the gunner jumped into the water, picked up his injured comrades, and carried them ashore. Having seen them removed to hospital, he sat quietly down on the beach, lit his pipe, and waited by the machine until help came to salve it. All this happened amidst the uncertainty of darkness and, so far as the actual landing of the machine went, with a Hun sitting overhead dropping bombs sniper fashion.

One pilot there was who determined to provoke a fight somehow, having grown tired of hawking into the Triangle and finding there no one who would come up and measure skill with him; so he flew down as low as he could at Zeebrugge and looped the loop along the Mole from one end to the other.

Even this contemptuous challenge failed to stir the enemy's fighting blood sufficiently for him to send a machine up. The challenger left Zeebrugge with "Archies" barking after him but no scalp at his belt, nor any chance of hanging one there. Neither did he suffer any damage, being in this respect more fortunate than a comrade, who during one of the numberless air attacks upon Zeebrugge had one hundred and fifty holes shot through his machine. In spite of this riddling he got it home safely, although the fabric of the wings was about as airtight as a sieve. Our machines, in fact, have a fine homing instinct; some way or another they manage to get back to their aerodromes when to all appearances they have been so badly cut up that they should not be able to fly at all.

Another illustration of this was the bomber which returned from a night expedition to Bruges with one of its lower planes so shot away that the fabric hung from it in big tatters like washing on a line. Disreputable as the machine looked after its night out, it had done a splendid bit of work against the enemy. Arriving over Bruges, the bomber found the barrage so strong that no way appeared open of breaking through it.

Carrying "eggs" home is a thing no "eagle" would think of doing, so the pilot of this one began dodging around in order to get a good shot at something. Whilst he was doing this the searchlights picked up the machine and held it. Though all sorts of manoeuvres were tried, the bomber could not wriggle out of their grasp. "Dirt" (as the airman calls shrapnel) was being thrown up in great quantities and the machine getting hit pretty freely.

Worst of all, a big shell struck it. Now the machine began to fly very strangely, and the pilot, still manoeuvring for attack, found himself barely a thousand feet from earth and below the searchlights at last. His back gunlayer, firing as rapidly as he could, knocked the "eyes "out of a couple of these, and this helped matters somewhat. Getting at last inside the defences, the pilot "yoncked" his bombs squarely on Bruges docks—a wonderful achievement considering the difficulties.

After doing it the bus staggered laboriously out of the whirl-wind of shelling loosed against it, scrambled somehow or other to four thousand feet (which meant danger all the way), and at this altitude flew home. Overhauled on arrival there, it was found that one of the propellers had been shot away and a plane torn to ribbons, as before described. Yet despite its crippled, tattered and torn condition, the machine flew—which, when you come to think of it, spoke favourably for the skill of the men and women at home who made the machine, as well as for the skill of the man who piloted it into action and out again.

War in its weirdest form is this night bombing, and nowhere quite so appealingly eerie as at Bruges. This quaint old Flemish city, strongly defended, pertinaciously attacked, will from hence-forward be as famous for its bombings as for its belfry. Here the Hun devotes all the energy he can muster towards keeping our airmen outside the place.

They try everything ingenuity can suggest to get into it. As a result of this thrust and parry the most unbelievable things happen over the town.

One bomber of ours trying to sneak in there was caught by the "onion" batteries, which began their detested jugglery of ball-play all around the machine. Somewhere about forty searchlights were stacked against him at the same time.

Try as he would, the pilot could not break through this fence; so he determined to attempt a new trick, in the very daring of which lay its prime chance of succeeding. Flying a little way in the Zeebrugge direction, he turned sharply back Brugeswards, shut off his engines, and planed silently down. A few seconds later the enemy gunners saw whizz past above their heads a big black object which strewed bombs quickly, then disappeared the other side of the town.

The conventional "before the enemy recovered from his surprise" would not be quite true here. So accustomed has the Hun become to our airmen doing unexpected things in the Hot Triangle that he is no longer surprised by anything. What is much worse for his nerves, he is a good deal worried as to what they will initiate next.

Straight for a canal basin one airman headed, dropping as low as possible in order to make sure. On the centre of the dock gates for which he was steering stood a Hun pumping out bullets from a machine-gun with terror-stricken energy. The pilot released his bomb, which struck its target fairly and up went Hun, gun, and dock gates, all mixed together.

Pilot No. 2 swooped in a second or two later and bombed the surroundings of the gates. It took the enemy quite a long time to repair damages. After he did this, what he put up was promptly knocked down again.

Such is the game of "skittles" as played by our airmen within the Hot Triangle all round the clock.

Going down quite low in order to reach an objective, though done frequently, has dangers unknown to the mere earthworm; one is that if the pilot be too near his target when he bombs it the explosion will probably turn his machine over. Many's the nasty bump adventurous wights have sustained in this way.

One pair of daredevils there were who whilst flying a two-seater one night came suddenly upon a big enemy anti-aircraft gun. The gun started firing at them when they were right down upon it, and they determined to blot the weapon out somehow. Determining is one thing—doing quite another. In this case the doing was particularly difficult because of searchlights and other things.

So low down were the pair when they attacked that the bomb explosions pitched their machine about like a cork on the waves. After a bit of rough voyaging they sailed gaily off again, leaving behind them only a smoking desolation where once a fair, bright "Archie" stood.

"Shooting up" searchlights seems a quite popular recreation with these air fighters of ours. But those who play it are by no means timid fellows; if they were, their record of work within the Hot Triangle would not be the brilliant chronicle it is.

Personal escapes of the strangest nature occur. One of the

most remarkable was that of a pilot whose machine being hit by a hot burst of shrapnel, a bullet entered at his sleeve, passed down his forearm and out at his wrist, cutting off his glove-buttons but hurting him not at all. Likewise individuality crops out, as always it will.

The thing our flying men least believe in is going to war heavy-hearted; and the longer they have been at the game the more ready are they for any little humorous relief in the grim business.

American pilots, possibly because they are newer comers, incline towards going all out for blood. Down in the Triangle they show themselves determined fighters and fine hands aloft. Being in this respect on a par with our own aviators, both work together, feeling quite satisfied that one will not let the other down should "old man Hun" tight-corner them.

Daylight bombers are not supposed to fight except in self-protection—though they do—being provided with an escort to do all necessary attacking for them. One such squadron had attached to it an American pilot who, never having had a chance of "getting his Hun," was determined to take first opportunity of bringing one down. Whilst the squadron was busy bombing a certain objective a number of Hun planes showed up.

The American had peppered his target and was already streaming homeward when the enemy appeared. "Gee, I'm in this!" he joyfully decided. Pulling his machine round, he singled out a Hun and made for it. Quite a determined "scrap" followed between them, which ended in the Hun rolling over and falling in flames to the earth. The American had shot him down, and there was not a happier man than he in the victorious squadron when it reached home. He had battled and won; he was a full-blooded air fighter at last, and over his soul there lay a sublime content.

All the most strenuous air work in this sector does not fall upon the bombing and fighting squadrons. There are machines specially employed on anti-submarine patrol. Over the sea lies their beat. Particular knowledge and strong powers of endurance are necessary to the men who pilot them. Like all other airmen in this part, they have done splendid work.

Owing greatly to their vigilance the U-boats are unable to operate effectively off this coast, and many of these pests have been bombed out of existence. The photographic aeroplanes likewise come in for a full share of the rough labour within the Hot Triangle. After the bombers have visited a place the photographers must follow them there to make records of the results obtained.

This means long flights into enemy territory; frequently also sticking about above "hot spots" until the required picture has been obtained. Photographs are usually taken from a very high altitude. Going lower would be too dangerous—a fact which in itself conveys an idea of how exacting the task is. Air war offers no cushy jobs to those engaged in it, no matter what their vocation may be when upon the wing.

CHAPTER 14

The Guns in the Dunes

As the official reports of attacks upon Ostend and Zeebrugge have time and again announced, one section of the Dover Patrol consists of siege batteries posted on the Belgian coast, "The Guns in the Dunes," as they are called by those who have mutual relations with them. Whilst the name conveys an idea of the guns whereabouts it gives the merest inkling as to the nature of their surroundings.

Yet environment counts as a matter of importance everywhere along the Western Front. It makes all the difference whether one be on dry ground or in a mud-hole; whether underfoot be sandy or swampy; whether one has an ammunition-dump or a farmhouse for a near neighbour. By such apparently trivial circumstances as these the tenor of life is determined. Being next door to a dump may mean sleepless nights and days of turmoil; whilst in the vicinage of the farmhouse there broods the calm that should be habitual to a rural atmosphere. Farmhouses, unless on a battlefield, do not attract enemy attention. Dumps always do. That explains why the one is a pleasanter neighbour than the other.

Location counts as just as important a factor as contiguity. In this respect the officers and men who form the train attendant upon the lordly guns in the dunes are not quite heavenly circumstanced, though happy enough withal. All are Royal Marine Artillery men. They live, Arab-like, in a desert, for that's what "the Dunes" resemble at the present time. It's a mistake to picture these as just a few sand-hills. Standing in any of the valleys that furrow them one might easily imagine oneself in the Sahara.

From Malo, by Dunkirk, right along the Belgian coast there runs a broad strip of hummocky, billowy, insistent sand; capricious as woman in some ways; inexorable as Time in others. Though there can be no certainty of finding its aspect in any part alike for two days together one thing remains unchangingly sure: whatever the sand grips it holds, and will ultimately devour. Four years ago this frill to the North Sea was in process of being gradually trimmed down and dotted with little communities, who were not anchorites, although they did live in a desert. Now the rough hand of war has nearly obliterated all traces of human habitation.

The wilderness has reverted to wilderness once more, flecked here and there with pathetic ruins of those modern miniatures of Nineveh and Babylon—destroyed since the Hun raped Belgium—the shell-beaten walls of which are being slowly engulfed by the powdery white grains heaping up around them. In short, there are few attributes of the greater deserts which this smaller one lacks except it be their spacious aridity.

Amidst this gritty solitude the siege guns and those who look after them hide cunningly away. So cunningly that one might walk over their lairs a dozen times unguided without suspecting what lay beneath. On every side one sees nothing but sand; here, barren and drifting, being continually scooped into big hollows or piled into miniature mountain ranges by the wind; there, patched with a scrubby vegetation struggling hard to exist, and only partially succeeding. This belt of lonesomeness is the favourite playing-ground of the sea wind which romps merrily about tossing the sand in all directions, imitating a monsoon one hour and a sportive summer breeze the next.

Of all the discomforts this is the worst.

It is impossible to get away from wind-blown sand. The gunners have built themselves wonderful quarters in its unstable bosom. But shore up and close up as they may, they cannot shut out the drifting particles. These filter through everywhere. Always there is sand on their mess-tables, peppering their food untastily, sand in their eyes, their ears, their mouths, and their clothing. Sand even goes to bed with them. Yet despite all this a healthier, cheerier lot one could not find.

Any visitor whom a wind of chance blows along in that direction may be sure of a hearty welcome to the burrows in which they live—for burrows these really are.

Weird sort of places even to any one accustomed to dugouts. In response to a genial "Come in and make yourself at home" you slip through an aperture into a cramped space that may be screened off at the entrance by a strip of canvas, or may be wide open to the desolation outside. It does not greatly matter which, as sand follows you in and keeps paying friendly calls upon you all the time you stay. As one covering of it is swept off the table another deposits there.

"Hang it all, let the stuff alone," says one of your hosts to another who tries to keep the table clear. "It will come in, you know, and we're so used that we don't notice it anyhow. No good if we did. You'll get like a walking sand-bag, same as we are, if you stay here long," he adds with a happy laugh.

If you are not nervous you find the injunction to "make yourself at home" easy enough to follow, for sincere hospitality efficaciously salves discomforts. But if you be at all timid you are likely to have a jumpy time of it.

"Whing! Whuff!" sounds overhead, followed immediately by the noise of a muffled explosion quite near, so near that it seems just outside.

Although you recognize the sound as that of an incoming shell you ask instinctively, "What's that? "

"A five-nine," answers one of your hosts.

"It's a good way off," adds another.

As nobody else seems to take any notice of the matter you dismiss it also.

"Whing! Whuff!" and another muffled burst comes a minute or so later.

THE FOREFUNNEL OF THE *VINDICTIVE* AFTER THE FIGHT

"Rotten shooting," comments someone, whilst the subaltern with the teapot opines that "Fritz's right off it today," and calmly goes on filling teacups.

Curious to discover how far "off it" Fritz really is you peep outside and notice the smoke of the shell rising from behind the shoulder of a nearby sand-hill.

"But that's nothing," protests the subaltern who has followed you, teapot in hand. "This stuff" (a wave of the teapot here indicates the sand) "is a fine localizer of explosions. Shell's got to be right close before it gets you. Don't bother. There'll be a lot more coming in!"

As a concession to your novice's curiosity to see the "lots more "arrive the mess accompanies you outside, and unconcernedly finishes its tea there whilst watching the Hun shells fall.

Each one is "ticked off" by some such comment as "That's a dud," and "That comes from—" "He'll get our garden!" (This with real concern.) But never a flicker of personal fear does any gunner show.

Quite a number of the Hun projectiles prove "dud," for which you are thankful, not being so hardened to bombardments as your hosts. But knowing something of the hammerings they receive at times when the Hun has been worried up into a state of wrathfulness by their damaging assaults upon him you ask:

"What do you do when the shelling grows what you call really hot?"

"Scoot," comes the prompt answer. "Only a fool takes foolish risks. Fritz's biggest stuff could not hurt us once we're in cover."

Nevertheless, the guns in the Dunes have had their share of casualties. The ingenuity of man cannot devise absolute protection against the freaks of shellfire, which are sometimes impishly capricious. Supposedly safe positions get crumped up, whilst the most exposed ones escape untouched.

This not being a subject upon which it is permissible to dilate, the housing of the big guns cannot be very fully described.

Rather a pity too, since few of the millions of people at home who are being fought for know anything at all about this interesting corner of the war. Anyway the weapons are well housed in subterranean forts wherein everything is spick and span, marvellously so, considering the surroundings.

From the C.O. down to the tail-end "number" each man takes great pride in the guns. The breech ends of the great pieces gleam like polished silver. Well they may. From muzzle to firing-key they are rubbed down and groomed as carefully as though they were thoroughbreds—as they are of their sort. Standing beside their long tapering barrels it seems hard to realize that from the hole by the seashore in which they hide, these guns can lob heavy shells into such far-off places as Ostend and Zeebrugge, places well outside the range of vision—but they do, and hit the mark every time.

Such is the business of the guns in the Dunes; to poke their grim muzzles this way or that as ordered, and suddenly drop death and destruction upon some enemy strong- hold invisible miles away, and they do it. If you would know how frequently or effectively ask the Hun. He is best able to answer the question. In one of these gun-pits in the Dunes an officer gives an order.

Thereupon somebody jerks the firing-key. A huge mass of flame and metal goes leaping up an embrasure (from above it looks as though a sand-hill had suddenly turned volcano), some few seconds later a building at Zeebrugge or men and guns elsewhere start disintegrating—little pieces going in all directions. The shell from the Dunes has blown them up. Weird and a bit marvellous too, isn't it? But only part of the Hell's-magic of war that works more strange and devilish wonders every day.

Of course the guns in the Dunes have to stand bombardments as well as give them.

The Hun is one of those aggressive persons who will not take anything lying down where they can get up and give a kick back. There may be two opinions about his expertness with some weapons; there can be only one as to his readiness with artillery. He is there with it every time. At least, on this part of the line. In addition to shooting often, he shoots straight. Though our gunners are his master, yet he manages to keep the air warm for them, and makes walking in the open oft-times a dangerous recreation.

With Hun shells daily in the air, and the desolation and discomforts of a desert all round them, how do the guns' crews pass their time when not actually fighting; in what way find relief from the strain? In the best manner of all; they have made them a garden. Situated in a little oasis of scrub, this garden keeps their table supplied with most vegetables—except potatoes. How the stuff grows or what it feeds upon remains somewhat of a mystery even to the gardeners themselves; for there is no soil, only bare sand.

Potatoes decline to put forth any increase in it; but other vegetables do well. Lettuce, beans, etc., stand up in thriving rows, whilst pumpkins of aldermanic rotundity loll comfortably in their beds. The men have made themselves not only a garden, but a very successful one. In tending it they obtain the best recreation possible, and also are following the instinct of their race by taming the wild, though on a very small scale.

Seeing few people, though otherways in touch with all things that concern them, the guns in the Dunes are a small though an important part of the Great War. Here land-front and sea-front meet, and these guns form the universal joint that connects the two.

CHAPTER 15

The Night Watch on the Brine

Sitting one evening at a window overlooking Dover Harbour I heard a lady exclaim in astonishment, "Why, all the ships have gone! "This was only relatively true. A good many craft still strained at their moorings; but the numbers had thinned down considerably in a very short period.

Without so much as a formal "May we part company?" they had cast loose one after the other and slipped out to sea. Destroyers, drifters, etc., disappeared along various courses. Each had its job to do, and went off to do it without making any fuss about the matter. Characteristic this of the navy all through. For that service never fusses over anything, least of all over the work on hand. It's "Get off silently and carry on—and mind that you carry on efficiently, or there'll be gold-laced trouble waiting for you on your return to port."

Our "Watch upon the Brine" is carefully organized. Patrols plough through blue water wherever that flows. But for obvious reasons they are more numerous in the narrow seas than elsewhere. Not a square mile in the Straits of Dover or on either hand of them goes unwatched, and in the dark hours the vigil is closest of all. The sentinel ships, after turning on to their course, plod steadily up and down it, no matter how bad the weather may be, until the time for relief arrives.

Travelling in a destroyer on night patrol is a picturesque experience. Lying in harbour, where larger hulls dwarf them, these craft seem only miniature vessels. Go aboard one and you get a different impression. You find that she is a real ship, well found and complete. Long and narrow, but with far more deck space than you had imagined. Routine is easier than in battleships or cruisers. This does not mean that work is lighter. Quite the other way about. Only in order to compensate for some of the discomforts more go-as-you-please ways are permitted.

When starting upon one of these night trips nearly every one changes into the least valuable clothes he possesses. The commanding officer, who came aboard in immaculate gold lace and spick-and-span uniform, climbs the bridge, sea-booted, with a thick muffler round his throat, wearing cap and jacket in which he would under no circum- stances be seen ashore. From Number Two down to the coxswain all follow the "skipper's" example, the reason for this being that if the smart "rig-out" remained upon its owner instead of going into "storage" for the night it would most likely be spoiled by the morning. Destroyer work tells heavily upon clothes as well as upon the men who wear them.

To reach the vessel's bridge you climb steep iron ladders. Stepping off these you come into a high-perched, circular, canvas-screened structure wherein are crowded several persons and a gun, together with a wheel, chart-table, and whatever else may be required for navigating the ship. The contents of the bridge will differ according to the type of destroyer. From this elevated post you obtain a bird's-eye view of the decks, and a wide visual sweep of the water all around them. Room for movement there is little, but by craning your neck over the rails you can see the remainder of the flotilla stringing out behind.

A fascinating picture they make dipping and rolling whilst the smoke pours from their funnels. Forward on the bridge the captain and the navigating officer carry on a monosyllable conversation in undertones, each keeping meanwhile a sharp lookout on either side. What they have to say deals wholly with the work in hand. Now it is a brief comment upon the dirty weather that is blowing up; again a question as to what some object sighted may be. Of general conversation there is none; not even as a concession to the "passenger." In fact, there is really no talking at all beyond what proves necessary, everybody being so fully occupied with his duties that he has no leisure for aught else.

As the bearded and ruddy-faced quartermaster spins the wheel about he quietly repeats the orders given him. The only time a voice is raised is when the man at the speaking-tube calls down it to ask whether a certain "number "of the after gun is at his post. Always the answer comes "Yes." But at intervals the inquiry is repeated, though not always addressed to the same individual. From each part of the ship keen, steady eyes are scanning the horizon. And the captain, as the responsible head, must be assured that all his crew are alert at their posts.

Gradually night deepens. Almost before you are aware of it darkness has covered the face of the sea. Instead of everything being blotted out by this as might have been expected, surroundings now become more intensely interesting. Over the Northern coast signs of battle begin to peep up. The flashes of the guns along part of the Western Front show quite vividly. At some points far off they are like the quick play of faint summer lightning.

Nearer, they blaze in darkness with broad yellow glares, and the dull "thud, thud" of their discharges comes beating across the water. After watching this for some time, you turn towards our own shores, mentally contrasting the peaceful serenity which broods over them with the rending, tearing war that tortures the night on the opposite side of this narrow stretch of salt water, and wonder, for the hundredth time perhaps, whether the British people really understand how much they owe to their never-sleeping navy.

"Hallo! poor old Dunkirk's getting it again " exclaims someone. Turning quickly in the direction indicated you see the sky above this much-bombed town constantly filling with the sharp bright twinkles of bursting shell.

"Archieing the Huns, that is," comments a seaman. "Air-raiders are goin' to be busy tonight."

He proves a sound prophet. Very soon there are ample evidences that air-raiders are very busy indeed. A brilliant constellation springs over Ostend. Soon there comes another above Zeebrugge. Then at various other spots in this part of Hunland the "fires of hate" leap upward. It is just as though you were viewing so many Crystal Palace displays.

"That's our machines givin' ole Fritz a shake up," the sailor explains. "An' they don't arf give it 'im neither. Nearly every night 'e gets it right in the neck like that. Wish we could get a chance at 'im too" (this quite wistfully), "but the blighter won't come out."

And there you have the sailor's chief grievance against the Hun, "the blighter won't come out." Nevertheless, the patrols must put to sea regularly and look for him in case he does make a venture. Sometimes their hearts are gladdened by the loom of destroyers in the offing. "Clang!" goes the engine-room telegraph for "full speed ahead." With eager anticipation each officer and man tautens at his post. But disappointment follows. The enemy has smelt danger and bolted back to his funk-hole out of its way.

A fairly common experience this on night patrol in these waters. The ships go out never knowing at what instant they may find themselves engaged with the enemy. Anything that does happen will happen on the instant. Therefore a state of constant preparedness is necessary lest one commit the unforgivable sin of being caught napping. And the strain of thus persistently hanging "on the top line "night after night tests endurance far more severely than actual fighting would do.

After what fashion is preparedness maintained? Let us go down from the bridge and see. By now the weather has beaten up rough. The destroyer rocks so giddily to and fro that descending the bridge-ladders in the dark is like climbing down the swinging pendulum of a clock.

Once on deck good sea-legs are needed. Even with these, progress is unstable. You must hang on to the life-lines or down you go. If you do go down you will most likely go overboard— and that will be the end of you, for there's no hope of being picked up. Remember, all around is inkily black. Except for the glow that comes from the engine-room—and that's battened down as much as possible—no lights show anywhere.

Feeling your way cautiously along you come upon one of the broadside guns. Beside it, standing immobile, you just discern the figures of men facing seaward. Were you able to pick out such details you would probably find that these men had tied themselves to their gun in order to keep foothold. These are the principal "numbers." Others of the gun's crew lie curled up close by, behind anything that will give them shelter from the water that every now and again jumps over the gunwale, and goes swishing across the decks to tumble off them on the opposite side. The recumbent men are not sleeping. A call to action would bring them to their stations before the words conveying it had been fully spoken.

Beside the searchlights are other silent figures each ready to promptly obey the command to "switch on." The torpedo-tubes, lying athwart-ships fore and aft, are similarly manned. So are the inboard guns. In short, it soon becomes apparent that the ship which seemed deserted above deck when you were looking down upon it is really alive from stem to stern with braw-sinewed, alert men. The quiet overlying her is not the silence of sleep, but the silence of intent watchfulness—as would be quickly enough demonstrated if an enemy came within reach of her guns.

Feeling your way along, staggering under the lively movements of the boat but keeping sure handhold upon the lines, you are presently startled to notice two white-rimmed eyes staring at you from just below your knee. Stooping to investigate you discover these to belong to a stoker who has pushed up his head from a manhole to catch a breath of air. Except for the eyes and an ivory gleam of teeth as he smiles at you, his face is as black as the coals he shovels. With a deep-breathed inflation of the lungs he disappears.

You bend down and peep after him, but have no wish to follow. Above deck may be bad enough, below seems less inviting.

Yet down there are squads of men toiling mightily, in cramped spaces, amidst sweltering heat, to keep steam in the powerful engines that drive the destroyer along. But for their work, little noticed yet all-important, the guns and tubes above deck would be shorn of their fighting efficiency, since a vessel cannot manoeuvre unless her engines be in good trim.

So throughout the long hours of the night the patrol "carries on." In fine weather the task is less exacting, but for the greater part of the year rough weather is met with. Seas that break over the ship from end to end, drenching everybody, winds with a chilling Arctic edge on them, are a frequent experience. Whether the moon shines on placid water or Northerly gales are howling along the surface makes no difference. The patrol vessels must still go out and stick it through.

Although fortunate enough to have had a fairly good passage, the rosy face of Dawn peeping brightly over the horizon is a welcome sight to your eyes. For it means that the patrol has ended. The destroyer turns her weary head back towards harbour, there to "pipe down" until returning night calls her back to her "beat" again.

CHAPTER 16

The Navy's Bulldogs

Monitors move like snails and fight like bulldogs. A steam launch could outmanoeuvre them, but neither big guns nor little guns can chase them away once they are settled down determinedly to attack. If they draw off "voluntarily" they soon go snarling back and fix in their teeth again. The earliest use of monitors during the war was in connexion with the Dover Patrol, where they quickly justified the revival of what had been regarded as a hopelessly obsolete type of warship. At first there were only two, these not of the best, judged by present standard. But they did most effective work against the enemy along the Belgian coast, where monitors have been continually employed ever since.

One of the originals, the *Mersey*, subsequently achieved fame by getting herself up as a floating island and in that guise smashing the German cruiser *Königsberg* in the Rufiji River. For this remarkable essay in camouflage the *Mersey's* decks were covered with earth and trees, whilst her crew coloured their hands and faces green so as to harmonize with surroundings. Only a monitor could have adopted such a guise. Broad decks and low freeboard permitted it. Only a monitor could do what monitors are doing daily off the shallow, difficult seaboard of Flanders.

Their light draught takes them where no other heavy vessel could float. From a single pair their strength in the Dover Patrol has grown to a squadron. Design has improved as numbers have increased.

A monitor is still a freakish-seeming craft. She has no beauty of colour, none of the aggressive stateliness of a Dreadnought. She looks what she is, a doughty, bull-necked fighter, with no pretensions to gracefulness either of form or movement. Her gait is something between a wallow and a waddle: her hull a broad, low, oval platform with an armoured citadel containing guns big and little, and surmounted by a tripod mast, sticking up in the middle of it. Big, corpulent "blisters" bulge out all along her sides. She moves sluggishly, steers awkwardly, but reaches her goal nevertheless, and "plays hell" with the enemy when she gets there.

In one point she betters some other warships: there are spacious, comfortable quarters for the crew, especially in the larger class.

When bombarding along the Belgian coast monitors do not play a lone hand altogether. When one of them sets out from Dunkirk there goes with her a swarm of small craft that makes the monitor, looming big in the midst of them, seem like a mammoth duck with a numerous brood of young swimming round her. Ahead steam a flotilla of destroyers, coastal motor-boats skim along inshore, whilst a string of motor-launches plod with steady pace abeam. Satellites all of them, each with its special duty to do.

Off Zeebrugge or Ostend the monitor anchors by the head, to keep herself in position, and lies with her bows pointing shoreward. In this position she offers such a small target to the enemy that the gunner of his who hits her, unless by accident, must be as good a marksman as William Tell. All of her that shows above the water is the citadel and mast. At many miles distance these appear about the size of a broom-stick when they can be seen at all. Usually they cannot. Contrary to what might be supposed, a bright sunny day is not esteemed good "bombardment" weather.

A misty atmosphere with "low visibility" is preferred, for then the monitor can get closer inshore and lob her ton weights of steel on to the target more effectively. If Father Neptune is not obliging enough to provide a real fog, the motor-launches create one artificially. They specialize in making smokescreens amidst which the monitor can hide from the enemy gunners.

Steaming between the ships and the beach the launches start the smoke rolling in dense volumes with the special appliances they carry for that purpose, until it quickly makes a thick impenetrable wall. Not a pleasant job "smoke-making," as anyone who has inadvertently swallowed a mouthful of the "fog" will agree. But the launches keep the screen going—and the monitor gets going also.

"Stand by for the buzz," orders her captain. Everyone on the bridge stuffs wool into his ears or covers them with pads to deaden the sound. "All ready "is reported from the gun-house. Those around the captain watch him, anticipating what he will say, and press the tips of their fingers to their ears as he gives the command "Fire!" Instantly the upward-pointing mouth of one of the big guns spits out a broad, blinding, yellow flash and a huge puff of acrid smoke.

Amidst this combustion is a shell which you cannot see, though you can hear its shriek dying away into the distance if you unclose your ears quickly enough. Well plugged though your ears be the detonation of the gun causes a sharp stabbing pain in them, and the shock makes you stagger, for the ship reels beneath your feet under the force of the concussion. "'Tween decks" doors bang, furniture pitches, the mess-traps go clattering all over the place, glass and crockery suffer heavily unless carefully stowed beforehand.

Once at least a tasty dinner cooking for the ship's company and almost ready for serving was thrown out of the galley and strewn on the deck. What the ship's company said when they saw this happen it's useless to repeat here, since it would not pass the Censor. Sometimes after strenuous bombardment a monitor's upper deck-plating becomes so buckled up that it resembles a badly laid carpet. From this effect of big-gun fire upon the place where the shells start from one may judge somewhat of its effect upon the enemy within the place where the shells explode.

The gun's crew inside the barbette feel discomforts of the firing least of any. And those outside are so accustomed to the concussion and what results from it that they pay small attention to either. Far up in the sky sits an aeroplane observing the fall of the shot. As this drops the "spotter" signals back information. "What is the report?" asks the captain.

From somewhere inside one of the bridge structures a voice answers him. It may be that the round was a "short" or an "over." Possibly some right or left deflection has to be allowed for. Necessary corrections are made and the gun roars out again.

"Ringed it that time. What'll you have, a china ornament or a cigar?" facetiously queries the observer aloof.

This method of reporting may not be strictly regulation, though it's just as informing as if the most cut-and-dried formula had been used.

Quite likely the answer goes back in the same strain.

The British fighting man is the most humorous person in the world. He keeps up his spirits that way, recognizing that a joke is the greatest easer of burdens that can be found.

Having "got on" to her target the monitor continues steadily pounding away at it. All that one could see of her from a distance would be dense black fog amidst which gun-flashes every now and again show luridly. From the vessel's bridge it appears as though she were firing promiscuously over a thick cloud-bank that obscures the shore—yet each round is carefully directed and accurately aimed. Presently the Hun starts firing back. He cannot see the monitor so he endeavours to "straddle "her by throwing salvos through the screen at the point where he judges her to be.

Often he proves a good guesser too. His shells "plonk "into the water all round about. Sometimes they get so near that the monitor is obliged to shift her position. Along this stretch of sea-front the enemy pits naval gun against naval gun. We send ships' guns off the coast to attack him, and he brings up ships' guns inside the coast to defend himself. Naval weapons have a longer reach than land artillery, and here the Hun uses the best kind he possesses.

Consequently, when our monitors go along shore to bombard him they find themselves opposed to a long-reached, hard-hitting antagonist, who tries his best to give back blow for blow although it is always he who gets the black eyes and the bruises in the end.

Whilst the game of bowls is being played between monitors and shore guns, the destroyers keep watch lest any enemy torpedo craft make an attack upon the fighting ships. One can never be sure of what the Hun will attempt, so the only safe way is to make provision against everything. That's what is done.

Now and again he makes experiments. These are generally in the nature of giving old ideas a new opportunity. In this war pretty nearly every old weapon devised since the Stone Age and every new one that could be thought of were tried without getting things much "forrarder" for a wearying long time. The Hun, greatest pirate of other men's brains that ever was, has brought out many "gadgets," hardly one of them of his own invention.

Failing to keep them off him in any other way he suddenly brought out against our monitors a launch armed with torpedoes and controlled from overhead.

But this venture failed. The launches were sunk and what was overhead came down. Besides, it's a foolish waste of war energy to torpedo a monitor; she minds that no more than an elephant would having a handful of boiled peas thrown at him.

If a "tin-fish" merchant in the shape of an enemy submarine manages to get in a shot, the torpedo merely strikes a "blister" and explodes harmlessly. But the odds are ninety-nine and three-quarters against that particular merchant ever doing any more trade. The anti-submarine gunners on the lookout from every part of the ship's deck are almost certain to get him. It is the same with the occasional Boche aeroplanes that come out for bombing.

Special guns on the citadel never cease peering skyward for these machines, which have an option between turning back or being shot down. Usually they have the Hun-sense to choose the former.

Looking at the matter from the enemy's point of view, what's the use wasting machines and submarines against ships that regard being bombed as a very mild excitement and torpedoed as a comic incident in the day's proceedings! But shells are shells-when they come from a fifteen-inch gun. Nothing is ever left smiling after they've hit it. And upon shells the enemy relies mainly in his defence against monitors.

He seldom hurts them for he seldom hits them. Not having her stolid resisting power, the small craft which accompany the monitors get worried far more than she does. A direct hit would simply wipe one of them clean away. Though such an occurrence is very rare, it is common enough for very light craft to get "shaken up" by projectiles falling into the water close by them.

Motor-launches do quite a lot of hard work in connexion with these bombardments. Also much hazardous and gaspingly uncomfortable work—especially "fog-raising." When conjuring up smokescreens—or imitation fogs that better the real article-the motor-launches' crews have to stay amidst the asphyxiating abomination they are creating and take their chances. But they do not appear to mind this in the least. Most of them are "hostility blokes." That is, have joined the navy for duration of the war, and they have apparently concluded that one might just as well be suffocated as die of old age.

If a launch gets cracked up by a Hun shell and has to be lifted on to a monitor's "blister" for "first aid," as happens sometimes, the matter doesn't seem to worry the crew. After the "dressings" are on, they take her back to port somehow, and get ready for the next "shoot." "Old duck "monitor, of course, has to keep a motherly eye upon her swarming brood all the time "Hun stuff" is flying around amongst them, and be ready to give help when necessary. They may not often need it, but it must be there when they do. And that is another addition to the monitor's activities and responsibilities. She must do a certain amount of fending as well as fighting.

In the coastal motor-boats, or "scooters," Youth sits at the helm and faces everything. These are the most nimble of all the monitor's satellites. Hither and thither they scurry, and much too quickly for the enemy to hit them—though he is always trying to do so. "Plash "comes a shell into the water. With a twist of the wheel the "C.O." has sent the "scooter" flying out of the way. Another turn and she has changed course again, probably to go leaping along right inshore.

Beside the "C.O." sits his observer; crouched beneath the deck in front of him sit the engineers. These have about the most uncomfortable post of any engineers in any ship that floats—or skims either. For want of room to do aught else they have to sit doubled up beside the machinery, whilst a tabloid hurricane gallops over their backs, and all the water coming in "forrard" falls upon them. Here, chin upon toes, they sit and work, keeping the boat's speed up. Very useful auxiliaries in many ways are these "scooters "to the monitors during a coastal bombardment, and also one of the most picturesque features of her entourage. From her bridge, as they speed about, they appear to be just so many waterspouts moving rapidly over the surface.

The general conception of Belgian coast bombardments differs widely from the actuality. It is not the case of a captain deciding that because the day is fine he will take his ship and have a shot at the Huns. The firing has to be organized just as carefully as other parts of the Patrol's work, and all necessary craft provided for carrying it through. When the monitor at last returns to harbour with lightened magazines she will have done something more than hurl a few tons of steel at the enemy. These bombardments, which have an important place in the war activities of this area, are carried out at every possible opportunity, to the intense annoyance of the Hun, who likes them not at all.

CHAPTER 17

Twin Pillars of Sea-Power

Contrast ranks amongst the most effective forms of study. It puts up facts to tell their story one against the other, and so one learns truths without much labour of searching for them. By comparing Dover and Dunkirk, the two bases of the Dover Patrol, the pillars at the main gateway of our sea-power—one gets as illuminating a study of this kind as the world has ever provided. Dull and leaden-minded must they be who cannot perceive the lesson it conveys; stupidly indifferent to their own interests the people who neglect to profit by its teachings.

Bear in mind that one is not speaking here of places vastly remote from London. Dover is almost a seaport of the Metropolis. Dunkirk lies within some hundred odd miles of it, practically as close as Birmingham, Nottingham, and other familiar Midland towns. This nearness of the war is an important aspect of it which the British people have never fully grasped. War has rolled up to one of our frontiers, a jump of the "ditch" and it would be on us. Here is a situation pregnant with food for reflection; one well worth thinking out in all its bearings. Also Dunkirk once belonged to the British Crown until that amorous, cynical, and perpetually impecunious "Merry Monarch" Charles II sold the town to King Louis.

About Dover little need be said. So far as mere bricks and mortar go, it is a quiet picturesque town, nestling cosily in a pleasant valley. From the cliffs beside it a famous, ages-old castle turns a grim face seaward. The castle has seen many wars just

Officers of the Vindictive with their black cats

Left to right: Surgeon Payne, Surgeon Glegg, Commander Osborne, Captain Carpenter, Staff-Surgeon MacCutcheon, Asst. Paymaster Young, Gunner Cubby

as the hoarily antique church within its precincts has witnessed many upheavals of another sort.

Both castle and church still remain in the exercise of the functions for which they were built. And as fortress and place of Christian worship they bid fair to continue for centuries yet to come. The harbour beneath is full of war shipping. But though Dover lies right on the frontiers of the war—so near that it can hear the guns and at times see the reflection from them—the town, in a material fashion, has suffered hardly anything from war itself.

The famous white cliffs still smile a serene welcome back to the returning Briton. Sailor and soldier homeward bound hail them with joy as harbingers of the calm, sweet peacefulness of England, so different from the scenes of strife and turmoil he has left behind. But in Dunkirk, just across the "ditch," one sees another side of the picture, the other part of the combat, in all its instructive ugliness. What most strikes any person visiting this town for the first time under present conditions is its spirit of brave endurance.

This seems to be typified by the bronze Jean Bart, who stands in the principal square, still waving his sword defiantly aloft; a forceful, energetic figure that power- fully suggests what the attitude of a flesh-and-blood Jean Bart would have been at the moment. Peace be to his soul. Some one of his countrymen has had the genius to make a bronze model of this stout old sea-dog's soul, and set it up to become an inspiration and encouragement to the Dunkirkois in their hour of greatest need. In the sweep of his arm lies a gesture of triumph, a presage of victory sure to come.

Apparently that is how the Dunkirkois feel about the matter, for they lay as votive offerings at the feet of their hero such German aeroplanes as are brought down during the Huns' night raids in the neighbourhood. Quite a lot of the raiders fail to get home again. Wherever one may come down it is pretty sure to be at the foot of Jean Bart's statue next day, laid within a roped enclosure for all who wish to see. Around the "captive" gather the townsfolk, country people who have come in marketing, and the drivers of the British army vehicles parked along one side of the square.

Amongst them one hears such comments as: "That's th' blighter as come buzzin' low down over us last night. Winged 'e was, but 'e managed to 'op it out o' our way, so the French got 'im. Out at daylight they was looking for 'im."

In at least one case this was literally true. A Hun bomber, hit by one of our guns, struggled away in the dark with failing engines and fell at last in a field beside a canal where some French soldiers were out fishing. Promptly they seized it and advised their authorities.

At daybreak they were on the spot with the Mayor of Dunkirk amongst them, and a few hours later, the machine was on view in Jean Bart's square. Its three occupants were killed when the machine crashed. Fishing, by the way, is by far the most popular recreation hereabout. Dunkirk people seem to find in the gentle art a never-failing solace for their troubles. So do the French soldiers on leave. By sunrise one may see them along the quays dropping little circular nets and hauling these up again pulley-wise.

In the moats beside all the canals and amidst the reedy seclusion of the fosses around sleepy, mediaeval Bergues one comes continually upon anglers with an opened upturned umbrella strung from a pole in front of them. This is the creel into which their catch is dropped, and rarely do they use aught else. Fishing is a wonderful sedative for over-tired nerves.

No other recreation that man has discovered brings such peace to the soul or so surely induces that philosophic frame of mind that enables one to meet troubles with equanimity. And the Dunkirkois need all the moral stiffening they can obtain from any source whatever, for they have much to endure. Well does the town deserve the Croix de Guerre conferred upon it. In four years it has been raided from the air more than four hundred times, and its tribulations are not over yet.

Before the war Dunkirk was the Liverpool of Northern

France. Now it has gained fame as probably the most bombed town in any war area.

Very few fine nights pass without "Mournful Marie" (which gives notice of impending raids) emitting her tragic howl of warning. Then it's "Into the cellars all of you, and be quick about it." Most of the inhabitants will have gone there already; for in order to ensure a few hours' undisturbed repose the majority of them go to bed in early evening.

When darkness comes they leave their beds for underground shelter somewhere. About nine o'clock one meets them in groups making for these refuges. Neighbours gather at street corners and call to one another. When the customary party has collected they move off towards their "dugout," not dolefully, but chatting brightly. Some are jocularly discussing whether "*les Boches*" will really come; others animatedly discussing "*la guerre*" as reflected in the latest *communiqué* posted outside the Hôtel de Ville. Hun raiders may come and Hun raiders may go, but they cannot depress the brave French spirit, which knows so well how to meet danger with a smile, and, if it must die, prefers to die gaily.

Here and there mothers are calling their children who may have wandered rampartwards for a game, but are far more likely to be trooping along beside a party of British sailors or soldiers shouting "One penny, please!" These are the first words of English that the French children of the working class learn. And it is "Jack" and "Tommy" who gladly teach them. British sailor and British soldier, child-lovers both, are tremendously popular with French children because of the prodigal way they distribute pennies amongst them. It's "Here y'are, y' little beggar. Go an' buy some toffee!" or a commiserating "Poor little kids, rotten time they must have!" But always the pennies flow out. Often one sees "Jack" and "Tommy" rolling "coppers" along the Dunkirk sidewalks, delighted as the youngsters themselves at the joyful rush after the coins.

The little French girl seldom joins these scrambles. The woman's wit budding within her teaches her an easier and more profitable way than that. She stands by, sticks a finger in her mouth, peeps shyly and wistfully up—and gets pennies without the trouble of racing after them. For the great kindness of our sailors and soldiers to the French children there exists a psychological reason.

Most of these big-hearted fellows have little ones of their own at home, and when they make a French child happy it seems to them as though they were also gladdening the hearts of their own youngsters. Subconsciously they see, not the smiling faces nearby them, but other dearly loved rosy little faces in the England that seems so terribly far away. And how far away England does seem from a locality such as this, one must get into the war-shattered parts of France to realize. Everything is so utterly different from home.

"Gawd, what a place for people to live in!" exclaims Tommy, looking around at the scarred walls and windowless houses of Dunkirk. "Horrible, ain't it!" agrees Jack. And they are right. Dunkirk does not exhibit an attractive exterior. Enemy bombs have reduced the cathedral to a gaunt shell, whose shattered windows, broken arches, and violated shrines are an eloquent though mute protest against war as the Hun makes it.

Every street throughout the town has been damaged more or less—usually more. Great gaps yawn here and there. Houses stand without a window in them like so many peeled skulls with eyeless sockets. Such windows as remain are generally part board and part patched glass. Shrapnel-exploding bombs have pitted the house fronts from string-course to eaves as though they had been subjected to heavy machine-gun fire.

Uncountable thousands of these scars are spattered about the walls. In numerous instances the fronts are partially blown in. Damage is partially repaired somehow, and the occupants live in the uncomfortable interiors as best they can. Even were it possible to do that, substantial repairing would be useless, since what was put up in the daytime would probably be knocked down in the night.

Passing along the streets one comes constantly upon little

sandbagged apertures which lead to the underground quarters wherein the residents find shelter when the Hun is overhead, and most of them regularly spend the greater part of each night. Such as take their chance of remaining in bed sleep with ears wide open; as soon as "Marie" begins to wail, down to the cellars they go—as quickly as possible. The bombs that fall in Dunkirk are not a kind that anyone can treat with indifference. Added to which the noise made by the defences and the hail of flying shrapnel are both things to shelter from as much as possible.

Despite all this Dunkirk, though sadly maimed, is far from dead. Many of the people have left it. But some thousands still remain there and they "carry on" in the courageous unflinching French way that has won the admiration of all peoples except the Huns—and they cannot understand it, as it is so vastly different from what they expected would happen. Shops are open, so are the principal hotels, the cafes, and the public market. What is more, all do good business.

Take the difference between Dunkirk and Dover or any other English town and see what the contrast teaches. We owe our immunity from the crucifixion of woe suffered by the French base of the Dover Patrol, not to any forbearance of the Hun, but to the fact that he is unable to inflict such damage upon us though yearning soulfully to do so. Sea-power as personified by the Dover Patrol interposes a barrier which the enemy cannot pass.

Throughout the war sea-power has been our greatest imperial asset. Unquestionably the British Navy, of which the Dover Patrol is but a part, though a very important and efficient one, has been the greatest factor in saving civilization the world over from the onslaught of the modern barbarians whom the Kaiser and his War Lords have launched upon it.

To the British Navy we owe immunity from invasion; the food we eat and the continuance of trade that keeps us going financially. Without its protecting arm America could not have put her splendid troops in the field; neither could we have used the magnificent soldiery which our Overseas Dominions have raised. These are all things which should be remembered, not only now, but after the war is over. To forget them would be dangerous, for ours is a great Empire, and without it embraces sea as well as land in its firm, motherly arms it cannot be held together.

1.8.18

www.ingramcontent.com/pod-product-compliance
Lightning Source LLC
Chambersburg PA
CBHW031855090426
42741CB00005B/504